Object

Object

A MEMOIR

Kristin Louise Duncombe

ISBN: 979-8-9910741-0-0 Trade paperback
ISBN: 979-8-9910741-1-7 eBook
ISBN: 979-8-9910741-2-4 Audiobook

Library of Congress Control Number: TXu 2-438-744

Cover Photo by Daniel Attia (Getty Photos)
Book design by Glen Edelstein, Hudson Valley Book Design

Printed in the United States of America.

First printing edition 2024.

For Rose
And for girls everywhere

This is a true story. Some timelines and events have been compressed for narrative concision. Some characters are composites, and identifying details of many have been completely changed to protect confidentiality. Some conversations have been reconstructed. There are many moving parts in this story, many victims, and many layers of lapsed responsibility. I do not pretend to speak for anyone but myself, and the story that unfolded as *I* lived it.

This is my story.

Prologue

Abidjan, Ivory Coast 1982

You are twelve years old; it is dusk on a weekday evening, and your parents are drinking gin and tonics in the living room. The glass doors leading to the garden are wide open. The guards, their faces scarred with tribal markings, call their greetings to each other as they take their places in front of the diplomatic residences that line the street.

You are restless, unmoored, because Rose left today. The two of you have been connected at the hip since your family arrived in Abidjan two years ago. Your fathers were colleagues at the US Embassy, and your mothers, at your international school. But the real relationship between your families started with you girls. You were inseparable.

And yet, you have been separated.

You pick up a racquet lying in the grass. It is wet with dew, and droplets spray when you whack the tennis ball against the wall that separates your garden from the neighbor's. You take your loss out on the ball, backhand, forehand, backhand, forehand, gripping the racquet so hard your hand hurts.

Then your father says your name. He always sounds stern, even if he isn't, but you know to come when he calls. You drop the racquet and run to the house, stepping from the garden into the living room, the way you are about to step from the before of your childhood into the after.

"We have something to tell you," he says, in that same frowning voice. Your mother nods earnestly and points to her ears, as though saying, "You better listen!"

"There's a rumor going around. About Rose's father. Now that she's gone, we want to tell you."

Your mother wipes her eyes. "Such a lovely man."

"Someone made an accusation." Your father stares into his glass.

"A serious accusation," your mother adds.

The room tilts, and your heart thumps in your chest, so loud you can hear it. You lean against the arm of the sofa. Outside, cicadas sing.

"He's been accused of—"

"Bruce!" Your mother's tone is sharp. The ceiling fan turns in lazy circles. You hold your breath.

Your father rattles the ice in his glass. "There's been some sort of accusation … You wouldn't know anything about this, would you?"

CHAPTER ONE

Geneva, Switzerland 2016

I've applied for some money." I hovered behind Tano's chair at the dining room table. We had just finished dinner, and he was already back on his laptop studying the finances, as he had been prone to doing with a sense of urgency ever since we moved to Geneva six months earlier.

He didn't look up from the screen, so I sat down next to him, cleared my throat, and repeated, "I've applied for some money."

"What do you mean, 'applied for money'?" Tano turned toward me, looking confused.

"Funding." I handed him the document. "From Mount Holyoke." My alma mater provided money to alums every year to pursue further academic and creative work. "Depending on how much they award me, it may pay for our trip. Or at least part of it."

"What are you talking about?"

"The Great American Road Trip!" I tried to sound confident, pointing to the evidence scattered throughout the living room. *Fodor's, Lonely Planet*, and *Rick Steves* tomes on the United States were strewn across the coffee table. I had broached the idea a few months earlier, but it was entirely possible he had not taken it seriously, nor registered a word of the plans the kids and I had been discussing in his presence, for months, since then. And we had been doing *a lot* of discussing. Carmen, almost seventeen, had already identified a hundred quirky cafés and bookstores she wanted to visit, just by scrolling through Instagram, and eleven-year-old Lorenzo was rapidly coming up with his list of every skate park in America.

My anxiety flared. Tano often accused me of doing things without consulting him, but it sometimes felt impossible "consulting" someone who tuned so much out. He was the quintessential distracted scientist, absorbed in his own world. He didn't ask personal questions, not even the simplest ones, like "how was your day?" or "what are you working on?" which meant I had to bring things up, repeatedly, if I really wanted his attention. And since most things concerning the United States created controversy between us – in Tano's eyes, the USA was nothing but a disgraceful bully on the world stage – I was almost relieved by his disinterest.

"Just read it." The "application" was more like a book proposal. I was planning the Great American Road Trip because I wanted to write a memoir titled *This Land Is Your Land*, about discovering America through the eyes of my children, neither of whom were born there nor had ever lived there. But they had US citizenship (because I was American, even if I had been an expatriate for most of my life) and if asked, said they were American, too. But were they? Was I? What did it even mean to be American for people like us, who were always on the outside?

I studied his face as he skimmed the document. In his mid-fifties, he was still so handsome, with that dark, curly hair and salt-and-pepper beard. I had been wildly attracted to him once upon a time, but in recent years I had felt so lonely, so misunderstood, I couldn't even remember what it felt like to connect with him, sensually. And still, I yearned for his approval. His expression didn't change as he read. Then he handed it back to me. "You're trying to get them to pay for your vacation."

Ouch.

Even if he thought the premise of the book was a crap idea, he knew it had been a longstanding dream of mine to write it. To *write*, period. Or maybe he had tuned that out, too, after wearily accepting the publication of my first two memoirs, both of which spoke freely about our relationship and family life, including the discovery of his extramarital affair in the early years of our marriage. My need to write about that hadn't been driven by some tell-all revenge fantasy, but my desire to share how I coped. There were so many universal themes: Betrayal. Jealousy. Rage. Renewal. And all of that, far from "home."

But where was home?

That's why I wanted to write *This Land Is Your Land*, though Tano's suggestion that I just wanted a free vacation shook my confidence. It was hard to keep my voice steady when I answered.

"I'm not trying to 'get someone to pay for my vacation.' I'm trying to offset the costs of the project. I thought you'd be pleased."

Finances had always been an issue between us. Tano was from Argentina, and he blamed the United States for the hyperinflation that had wreaked havoc on his country's economy in the late 1980s. He saw me as a product of that system, a "privileged American." Fair enough: I was American and privileged. But I was not profligate, a reputation he had assigned me years earlier when, in a matter of days, I charged a thousand euros to our credit card. It was right after I discovered his affair, ten days before Christmas, when we still lived in Uganda. I took two-year-old Carmen, and we fled—in our short sleeves and sandals—to Paris, where we were meant to have moved as a family months earlier. The AmEx charges were for winter clothes, boots, blankets, pots and pans, and some toys for Carmen.

Even though the expenses stemmed from his betrayal, Tano never trusted me thereafter with money. This wasn't expressed just by the comments about my "luxurious" tastes, but the way he cupped his hand over the keypad at the ATM while paying for dinner at a restaurant, as if I was a bandit just waiting to catch a glimpse of his code so I could steal the card and go charge a few things to it.

I started talking fast, as I was prone to when I got nervous. "Did you see I wrote the budget for four people? I know you won't be able to take the entire summer off, but I would love it if—"

"You want *me* to go to the *USA?*" He looked at me as if I had proposed something outrageous. "After Kunduz?"

In October 2015, the US Air Force, in a "targeted" airstrike, hit a Médecins Sans Frontières hospital in Kunduz, Afghanistan, killing forty-two civilians.

"What happened in Kunduz is terrible," I said, not bothering to bring up the thing I had insisted about, to no avail, for years: that it was unfair to hold an entire nation of people responsible for their government. That it was unfair to make *me* pay, though I had accepted to do so twenty years earlier when we fell in love.

Though we met in New Orleans, in graduate school, Tano had made it a condition of our marriage that we leave the USA and never live there again. For me, that meant separation from my parents and sisters, who had all settled in Maryland, and the weakening of an already tenuous bond with my homeland after my childhood overseas. Though I largely agreed with his political critique, I could no more change where I was from than I could change who had given birth to me, and his disregard for that left me feeling effaced. But I didn't want to lose him, and I was too naïve, too bruised from all the events that had led me to that point, to realize that this was not a sustainable situation, that the end of our story was being written into the beginning.

Instead, I tried to appeal to his family sensibility. "The kids are so excited about the road trip. It's all they talk about. And I've always dreamed that you and I would see Californ—"

"I won't give another cent of my money to the *USA*," he said, as though he was cursing. "And what kind of person plans a family vacation that excludes one member of the family?"

"But you're not excluded! I'm begging you to come!"

"You know my position on the USA."

I stared into his steely blue eyes. Twenty years we had been doing this. Images of our life together flashed before me like slides in a carousel: New Orleans to Nairobi to Kampala to Paris to Lyon to Geneva. I had followed him from place to place, fracturing my career while he grew his, caring for the kids alone for weeks at a time because of his travel schedule. And I hadn't just adapted; I had thrived with every reinvention, even though it was never easy for me. I didn't expect a medal, but a little recognition, a little compromise, would have been nice.

What kind of person was I?

A person who had finally been pushed too far.

"I can't live like this anymore," I said, a sudden rush of heat and fury surging inside me. "I want to separate."

I don't know which one of us was more shocked by my words. I had an automatic impulse to take them back, to smooth things over as I was wont to do. But he spoke first, his expression as rancorous as his voice.

"You've known my position since the day we met," Tano said. "In twenty years, I haven't changed!"

And it was true; he hadn't.

But I had.

I moved out of the bedroom that evening. As if telling him I wanted to separate hadn't been bad enough, I had to ask him to open the rickety futon in the spare room for me, even though he'd shown me how to do it many times over the years. *"Observa!"* he'd say, and I would pay attention—sort of. I had come to the marriage with formal training in learned helplessness. It was the model of my parents' relationship to just let the man do all the logistical stuff, and having grown up in the Foreign Service, I had spent the formative years of my life within a system that coddled its own.

Now I lay in the dark on the lumpy mattress, trying to calm my racing heart. I couldn't believe what I'd done, leaping from my marriage as though it was a building on fire. I vacillated between trepidation and, unexpectedly, exhilaration. The Great American Road Trip had suddenly become a great act of emancipation.

But I hadn't really planned on emancipating; I wasn't prepared!

Tano had been the primary earner our entire relationship, and I had never paid attention to our financial situation. Time and again I had said, "You manage the money. I hate thinking about all that stuff." As a result, I had no idea about any of our investments or savings. I had always worked, but as a self-employed psychotherapist before online therapy was the trend, my income had fluctuated with every move. It took time to build up a clientele, and here in Geneva, my practice was not even half full. Now I had blown up our marriage and was planning a voyage to the place he despised: I couldn't bring myself to ask him to release some funds for it, even if it was technically my money too.

Tears sprang to my eyes. Maybe he'd come around when the grant came through. *If* it came through. Oh God, it had to. Otherwise, had I ended my marriage over a fantasy?

I pounded my pillow. Why had I been so unorganized? Why hadn't I put money aside, some secret stash for a rainy day or another crisis? Why had I made any of the choices that led me to this very moment? What was *wrong* with me?

Between the anxiety and the hot flashes, I couldn't stand it anymore. I threw off the covers and tiptoed to the kitchen. It was just after 3:00 a.m. I heated some milk and went down the long hallway to my office. The moonlight cast a single silver beam into the room, and I stepped into it, as if I were a diva stepping into the spotlight. Then I lay down in the middle of the floor, the wood cool against my burning skin, and swept my arms and legs back and forth, like I was making a snow angel.

This grand, eight-room apartment in central Geneva was by far the most beautiful space we had ever lived in. The rent would be exorbitant and the size excessive for a family of four were it only for living purposes. But we had rented it so that I could run my therapy practice from home, in this beautiful study with hardwood floors and an enormous window overlooking the park.

My office.

Part control center of my life, where I went to earn my money, part identity stamp, an extension of me. I pulled myself onto the cream-colored sofa and rubbed my hands over the nubby fabric of the calming, earth-toned cushions. This is where my clients sat, across the room from my chair, a worn but beautiful grey fauteuil that I had found in an antique shop. Behind it, an oak bookshelf stored more books than it had room for, and the dog-eared memoirs that I regularly assigned sat in piles, waiting to be loaned out again.

I had never had my very own office, nor such a lovely one. From New Orleans to Nairobi to Kampala to Paris to Lyon, I had been forced to acquire a flexible vision of what it meant to be a therapist … and an even more flexible vision of what a therapy space should look like. Over the years, I'd had a mishmash of strange, sometimes barely suitable offices, which was the reason I had worked so hard to develop my professional reputation. If the therapy was helpful, the ambiance wouldn't matter so much—at least that's what I hoped my clients would think. This was the first time in my life I had a workspace that made me feel like a competent professional, and now I was putting it at risk.

I threw my head back to get the last drops of milk; then I contemplated opening a bottle of wine. But in the end, I decided against it and crept back to bed. Out of habit, I went straight to the marital bedroom, realizing my mistake as my hand touched the door handle. I snatched it back as if it had burned me and hurried to the guest room. Before I closed the door behind me, I stood still and listened. Sometimes Lorenzo called out in his dreams, exposing little snapshots of life at the skate park, spoken in French slang. Carmen also divulged glimpses of her life, flashes of giggly conversation, interspersed with pleas for the rights of animals and world peace. But tonight, they were quiet, leaving me alone with my dread of telling them that their father and I were separating.

I would not tell them right away. I was too scared, and what if a miracle happened and Tano and I found some way to reconcile our differences? I didn't really think we would, but I also didn't think I'd ever fall asleep, and then it must have happened, because suddenly the sun was in my eyes.

For a couple of weeks, we carried on like nothing had happened. It was easy; we'd never had shouting matches or blowout fights, though screaming, and stamping our feet would have been preferable to the silence and withdrawal that had been established as the only acceptable tenor years ago. We were already so emotionally disconnected; there was no reason to stop our innocuous family dinners and anesthetic evenings in front of the television. Sleeping separately wasn't even suspect; over the years, I had often slept in the kids' rooms when Tano's snoring or my insomnia got too bad.

But one afternoon as Carmen and I studied Google Maps and talked about the road trip, she said, "Did you and Pop … break up?"

Lorenzo was watching television in the next room, so I lowered my voice, hoping to keep him out of it. "It's just an in-house separation for now."

"What's an in-house separation?" Lorenzo paused his television show.

The three of us sat together on the sofa, and I explained that their father and I wanted very different things and had decided to stop being a couple, but that it had no bearing at all on our love for them. Lorenzo listened carefully and asked a few questions, then quickly went back to his TV program. This was not the end of the discussion; we would pick it up whenever he was ready. But Carmen's eyes welled with tears.

"Is it my fault, Mom? Because I want to go to university in England?"

She and Tano had been in a long standoff over her desire to study English literature in the UK, a place he considered as evil as the USA because of the 1982 war over the Falkland Islands.

"That has nothing to do with it." I held her tight while she cried, wanting to reassure her, though what I said was not entirely true. It incensed me that he was now disparaging Carmen's cultural affinity the way he had always belittled mine, and this had contributed to tipping me over the edge.

But I was done fighting about it. In our current circumstances, I just wanted to focus on keeping the peace—and keeping my wits about me, because I was panicking about money.

Since we'd separated, I had been paying attention to every dime, and if I was careful with incoming payments, would have a grand total of $10,000 in my account to spend on the Great American Road Trip. Which was no laughing matter, yet the sum seemed barely enough to rent us a car for seven weeks and cover gas, food, *and* lodging.

And I hadn't even purchased the plane tickets yet.

The grant. The grant. The grant.

Every day I chanted these words in my head like a prayer; it was my last hope to show Tano that I would pay for this venture on my own and that it was legitimately an interesting idea, not just some crafty ploy to get a free vacation. I had to believe it would come through for me.

I didn't get the grant.

I'd been expecting an email, so the sight of a singular, slim envelope with the Mount Holyoke logo caught me off guard. It was a Saturday morning, and I was on my way to the grocery store. I debated opening it only when I was back home, but I couldn't resist.

Dear Ms. Duncombe,
We regret to inform you … So many wonderful proposals … so
hard for the judges to decide … Application denied.

I shoved the letter in my bag and charged down the road to the store. *Don't freak out*, I told myself, even as I was overcome by that same feeling I'd once had as a kid, packing my bag during some silly tantrum and running away from home, realizing at the corner that I'd never make it on my own.

I moved through the grocery store, outside of myself, choosing apples and lettuce robotically, staring dumbly at the yogurt for so long that the stock girl asked if I was all right. I gave her a wan smile and grabbed the first thing I saw, thinking, *I'm not all right at all. I'm scared to death.* All those Starbucks drinks I had guzzled over the years, all the treats bought for the kids on the go, flashed like a neon sign in my head. At the time, it had just been pure fun, but oh how I wished now I could get back that money I'd spent on instant gratification. In a sudden jolt of awareness, I went through the aisles, putting back all the items I had loaded into my basket without even looking at the price: fancy olives, organic hummus, pre-sliced cheese. How much could I save if I just paid more attention?

I was in a daze for the rest of the day, getting meals on the table and laundry into the machine, thinking about money and being in charge—or not—of my own life. My mind kept circling back to that terrible winter of Tano's affair and the thousand-dollar credit card bill. Overwhelmed by his reaction, I asked my parents to float me some money until I found work. Paris was expensive, and I still needed plenty of things to get the apartment into a more livable state. My father had written back saying they would be happy to send me the money, on the condition that if within six months I had not found a way to support myself, I would come home.

I'd never forget that initial desperation—*how am I going to manage?*—compounded by sudden clarity: *I have to solve this on my own.* I scrambled and found myself an under-the-table job managing tourist rentals, and within days of having asked for help, I told my father that I was retracting my request.

Into the evening, I thought back to that moment. It had foreshadowed my current situation; a sort of practice run, it seemed. *And if you figured it out at thirty-two*, I told myself, *you can figure it out at forty-six.*

I would trim the budget for the trip itself, replacing nice meals in restaurants with improvised meals from the grocery store, comfortable hotels with camping. I scrolled online late into the night, looking at cheap tents and inflatable mattresses, fighting the thoughts that kept bashing into my consciousness like a bird flying into a window pane: *I am a terrible person for leaving my marriage, the Great American Road Trip is a dumb idea, our plane will probably crash, or there will be a horrible car accident . . .*

"Stop it!" I hissed, pinching my arm, aware that I was catastrophizing, wasting time instead of doing something productive, like getting started on the book I'd blown up my life over. It suddenly felt urgent to get something, *anything*, down on paper, to quell my self-doubt and get me back to that moment when I still believed I had a great idea. *This Land Is Your Land* would be a poignant but funny collage of observations about three Americans, in varying degrees, discovering their country together. It would be a lighthearted but deep exploration of what shapes identity and sense of self.

I pulled up a blank page and typed:

THIS LAND IS YOUR LAND—Draft 1

Then I sat there, the screen mocking me. How would I write that book when nothing about my plan felt funny or lighthearted at all? I combed my mind for justifications; I had to believe my quest to write a book about discovering my country was worth all the upheaval. But the minutes ticked on, and I couldn't think of a single thing to say. My heart jumped in my chest, scared and wild. I didn't yet know that I wouldn't discover much about my country on this trip, but I would find something more fundamental: myself.

CHAPTER TWO

Abidjan, Ivory Coast 1979

Dad announced we were moving to West Africa the same week a stomach flu swept through my fourth-grade class. I avoided catching it, but after witnessing a kid throw up all over himself in the cafeteria—sour spaghetti and corn dripping down his shirt—I became convinced it was only a matter of time. While the rest of the family focused on the move, I obsessed about getting sick.

"I can't eat that," I cried, burying my face in a napkin one night a few weeks after the vomiting ordeal. My mother had just served me a plate of roast chicken and rice, something I would have normally eaten without issue.

"You've got to eat something!" she pleaded. It was the third time that week I had refused to touch my dinner, terrified that eating would lead to throwing up. There was only one "safe" food—applesauce—and Mom sighed as she spooned some into a bowl. "This isn't healthy! You're going to end up with rickets!"

When we went to the State Department medical center to get the many vaccinations required for the move, Mom told the doctor, "She thinks she's sick! It's crazy!"

He listened to my heart, looked down my throat, and said, "You're fine, dear." Then he turned back to my mother. "She's just worried about leaving her friends."

But I didn't have many friends in the leafy DC suburb where we lived. I was the kid that other kids made fun of because of my short hair (*"Everyone says I look like a boy, Mom!" "Well, tell them it's a Dorothy Hamill cut! Do they think Dorothy Hamill looks like a boy?"*) and ineptitude in dodgeball. A series of recurrent tics—madly blinking my eyes, or opening and closing my mouth in wide, ritualistic patterns—had not helped.

Mom implored me to stop making all those weird faces, and when that didn't work, Dad tried to command it. "Stop that! Now!"

But I couldn't. My face begged to be contorted, my eyes to be rolled, three to the left, three to the right, until I gave myself a headache. In those days, no one knew about OCD, or emetophobia, or childhood anxiety, in any clinical form. I was just weird.

It was a lonely time.

I was a lonely kid.

And I longed for someone to care that *I* was leaving, the way neighbourhood friends had my parents over for a farewell coffee and Sara Lee cheese Danish. The way my little sister's preschool organized goodbye cupcakes. The way my big sister's friends threw her a surprise party, presenting her with a package to be opened on the airplane. The night we flew out of Dulles airport, I oozed with envy as I watched her unwrap an autograph book with a red checked cover filled with messages from twelve girls, written in cherry scented magic marker.

Though I wasn't leaving a group of friends behind, that didn't mean I was happy to start over on a whole new continent. "Why did we have to move?" I moaned, pressing my face to the window of the DC-10 as Washington became a speck below us.

"You know the answer," Dad said impatiently; we had gone over it many times. He had joined the Foreign Service because he knew it would provide a better life for the family than his teaching career at Georgetown University ever would. My incessant calls for reassurance were certainly irritating, but I felt hurt, alone.

When we touched down in Abidjan many hours later, we were greeted by another diplomat who had come to the airport in an "official" car, an enormous white Land Rover, driven by an embassy driver who called Dad "*Monsieur,*" and Mom "*Madame.*" Traffic moved slowly as we made our way into the city, giving us the chance to observe the chaotic scene outside the window. People with bundles on their heads and babies on their backs streamed in either direction along the roadside. There were rows of food stalls, where groups of men shook hands and laughed while women braided each other's hair, gossiping over the music that poured from scratchy transistor radios. We rolled down the windows and the tang of sweat and dust and sun-ripened mangos came through, until the driver told us to roll them up when three small boys in filthy, torn clothing put their hands inside the car, asking for money with wide, toothy smiles.

Our house, in a wealthy neighborhood called Cocody where Ivoirian politicians and diplomats lived, came with staff who were there to greet us when we arrived. Emmanuel was a young man from Benin, employed as the "houseboy" to take care of all domestic drudgery. The guard, Moussa, was from Burkina Faso, and doubled as the gardener, caring for the lush garden that might well have been a royal carpet leading to the front door.

"Not shabby," Dad said, looking around the house. "Not shabby at all."

"It's wonderful!" Mom said, sinking into the plush sofa.

My sisters and I tumbled through the house, opening cabinets and closets and bickering over who would sleep where. When we spotted a gecko on the ceiling, we screamed and ran back to our parents in the living room. "The house has lizards!"

"They're harmless," Dad said, pointing to another one. "You'll get used to them."

"What if they bite us?" my little sister asked.

"Don't be so stupid," I said, even though I had been wondering the same thing. "Dad said they're harmless. Right, Dad?"

Suddenly, Emmanuel came to the living room. "*Le dîner est prêt, Monsieur.*"

"Girls?" Dad gestured for us to follow him to the dining room, where Emmanuel stood by the table, holding a platter heaped with spaghetti and meatballs. It seemed he was planning on serving us like a waiter, but Dad told him we could serve ourselves. He retreated to the kitchen and a few moments later, we heard music coming from the radio. Mom whispered, "Is he going to just wait there until we're done eating?"

Dad looked bemused. "I think so. Shall we?" He served both of my sisters and then he looked at me. "Are you eating?"

I had refused most of the meal on the airplane, except the dessert, and I was suddenly ravenous. I held up my plate, and Mom clapped. "Thank God!"

The Ivory Coast, once a French colony, gained independence in 1960. Because of the ongoing influence of its former colonizers, the capital, Abidjan, was still known as the "Paris of West Africa." Businesses owned and operated by French families dotted the city: *fromageries* with every cheese you would expect to find in France, *boucheries* where French men stood behind the counter and prepared cuts of meat, and *boulangeries* that sold hot, crusty baguettes, delicate pastry, and buttery, flaky *pain au chocolat.*

These French elements stood in sharp contrast to the other new realities that shocked our pristine sensibilities. We gasped the first time we saw the buckets of snails, plump and slimy, for sale at the Cocody Marché, and at the sight of Moussa knocking a black mamba from the tree in our front yard, hacking it to bits with his machete.

My tics and obsessions might have worsened in the face of all these changes, but the opposite happened. My little sister was the first to point it out. "You don't move your mouth in a funny way anymore."

We were sitting on the patio on a Saturday morning, finishing our breakfast. Cheerios were a thing of the past; in Abidjan, we ate *croissants* and *brioches*, washed down with glasses of fresh, syrupy pineapple juice.

"What do you know?" Dad looked at me. "It's true. I can't think of the last time you made a face."

I smiled, pleased to be noticed.

"Must be all the pastry we're feeding you," Dad joked, but I didn't laugh. It wasn't the first time a nervous tic had disappeared; it would only be a matter of time before my obsessive-compulsive tendencies came back. But for now, I was relieved. School started in a few days, and all the funny faces and twitching had always set me apart.

My parents had enrolled my sisters and me at the International School of Abidjan, where Mom had also been hired as the school librarian. On the first day, we discovered the school wasn't in an actual school building, but a house that had been co-opted for a campus, lending to the surreal, magical quality of our new lives. The student body was small; there was only one class per grade, and most grades only had ten to twelve students. My fifth-grade class was big, because there were sixteen of us, but already this made for a less intimidating environment than what I'd left behind in the United States.

The teacher assigned me a seat next to a smart-alecky girl named Rose. With curly red hair and a smattering of freckles across her face, she reminded me of Pippi Longstocking. Though we were both ten years old, Rose was savvier than me, accustomed to being part of this expatriate subculture. She had lived in the Ivory Coast for a full year prior to our arrival, and before that, the Philippines, on account of her father's role at the US Embassy.

One Friday morning, at the end of our first week of school, she waited for me at the front gate. "You want to see something?" She spoke in a low tone, leaning close to my ear in a way that made me feel like an insider. "Follow me."

We walked toward the back of the yard, Rose glancing around as if we were being watched. She stopped in front of some bushes, verdant against the mud-brick wall that surrounded the school. A large stick was propped to the side, as though someone had placed it there, and she used it to part the foliage closest to the ground. "Do you see?"

It only took a moment for my brain to register that it was a dead snake, camouflaged in its resting place, an army of ants profiting from its decomposition. I jumped backward. "Gross!"

"No one knows it's here." She lowered her voice to a whisper as she poked it with the stick. "Don't tell anyone, OK?"

"I won't," I said, thrilled to be in on this classified information.

She held up her hand. "Pinky promise?"

I linked my finger to hers. "Pinky promise."

We didn't unhook our fingers as we skipped, feet in unison, back toward the schoolyard.

School ended every day at noon, and we lurched home with Mom, who had only just learned to drive a stick shift. Dad came from the Embassy to join us for the delicious meals prepared by Emmanuel. When we were done eating, he took care of cleaning up while Mom and Dad had coffee in the living room.

"How lovely," Mom would sigh, kicking off her sandals, wiggling her toes. "I feel so spoiled. It's like being a child!"

This was an apt analogy, because "Ask the Embassy" or "We better tell the Embassy" was as common parlance as "Ask Mom" or "We better tell Dad." It was as though the Embassy itself was running the show. Like Dorothy, the Lion, and the Tin Man, who believed the Wizard of Oz to be the only one capable of solving their problems, the Embassy trained people to not look for outside solutions. Not only did the Embassy determine housing, neighborhood, and how long you got to stay, it was also in charge of the minutiae of daily life, such as changing lightbulbs and hanging artwork.

All of this in exchange for an oath to serve and defend the US government's foreign policy. I had no awareness of this obligation until fifty-two American diplomats were taken hostage at the US Embassy in Tehran. In the weeks following the hostage crisis, Dad worked late, and even on the weekends: Tehran may have been thousands of miles away, but the hostage crisis concerned all US diplomats and their families, because there could be copycat strikes.

It was hard to understand. Rose said the captors took the hostages because President Carter had allowed the shah to get treated for cancer in the United States.

"Why is that such a big deal?" I asked Dad one evening as he mixed a cocktail.

"It's complicated. Their new leader, the ayatollah, is angry with the United States."

"With the entire country? Like, even with Grandma and Grandpa?"

He quartered a lemon and smiled. "Angry with the government, not specific people."

"Then why did they take hostages?"

"Because the hostages work for the government. So, they represent policies of the United States that many Iranians disagree with. By holding the diplomats hostage, they can fight back against the things they're angry about."

"Well, why don't the hostages just tell them they agree? If they held me hostage, I'd say, 'I hate those policies, too! So let me go!'"

I was expecting him to congratulate me for this clever solution. Instead, he said, his voice grave, "That would be treason."

OBJECT

For weeks after the siege of the US Embassy in Tehran, I lay awake at night, worrying about Dad being taken hostage. I imagined him tied to a chair, defending the USA until the bad guys killed him. I whispered bargains, the air conditioner my only witness, that I wouldn't fight with my sisters or create a ruckus of any sort. But then daytime would come, and I'd forget. When that happened, I'd send myself up and down the stairs, in sets of four, chanting *sorry, sorry, sorry, don't take Dad hostage.* Nobody noticed my new ritual—it wasn't obvious like the facial tics—and I enacted it freely until it, too, phased out as the adults stopped talking about the crisis all the time.

The Embassy in Tehran was still under siege, but life in Abidjan went back to normal, and there wasn't much to worry about. Work, school, after-school activities a few times a week at the Hotel Ivoire, the five-star hotel that was home to restaurants, a movie theater, an enormous swimming pool, a bowling alley, and the only skating rink in all of Africa. Rose and I did all of our activities together, and when there wasn't anything scheduled, we hung out at her house. It was way more fun than mine. The Mulcahys stocked their kitchen cupboards with Oreos and candy corn and Betty Crocker frosting. You could buy all that stuff at the Embassy Commissary, but my parents never did. They were always watching their weight. At Rose's, we just helped ourselves to whatever treats we fancied and didn't have to share, unlike at my house where my sisters were always butting in.

Rose had five siblings, but they were in college in the US. Her sister Meg had just moved back to the States and had left behind all of her cool albums. She'd taped a sign on the box: PRIVATE PROPERTY. DON'T TOUCH. AND THAT MEANS YOU, ROSE—but we didn't pay any attention.

We danced to our favorite songs, dressed up in Rose's mom's old cocktail pantsuits, pretending to be rock stars. "Hot Child in the City" was Rose's, "Shadow Dancing" was mine, and we both loved the entire

Grease album. But our favorite song of all, we both agreed, was "Crocodile Rock."

The name of Elton John's album—*Don't Shoot Me, I'm Only the Piano Player*—gave us the idea for the book we were writing, because we were going to be famous authors, just like Judy Blume. Our story was about a boy named Calamity Collision who kept getting into accidents and messes. Every time he did, he'd say, "Don't blame me, my name's Calamity."

This was also the title of our book, though we referred to it in shorthand as just Calamity Collision.

Over time, the thickening stack of pages covered in my messy, looping handwriting and Rose's, neater and compact, was as exciting as the story we wanted to tell. It already looked like an actual book, kind of. There was a grease stain on the cover where Rose had put her grilled cheese down, and page twelve was all smudged from when I spilled my water, but the pages made that delicious crinkling sound when you turned them, and it was even divided into chapters.

"Do you think we should include pictures?" Rose asked one day as we floated on our backs in the pool at the US ambassador's residence, across the street from my house. The pool was open to the Embassy community, but only a handful of people used it regularly—namely my family and the Mulcahys—so it was almost like having our very own private pool, tucked at the far end of a sprawling garden, behind a wall of hibiscus and bougainvillea.

"You mean like illustrations?"

Rose flipped over on her stomach and swam a few strokes. "Yeah. We can draw them ourselves."

I was about to agree with her idea when Mr. Mulcahy stood up from the chair he'd been sunbathing in. "Guess what I am!" he shouted, waving his arms and making a weird face.

Rose and I treaded water side by side, looking at him and giggling.

"What-ah-yah, stoopid?" He waved his arms even harder. Then he jumped in the water with a big splash. He came up sputtering. "I'm a duck!"

Mr. Mulcahy didn't look like a duck. He looked like a frog, an albino man-frog, with puckering lips and clear eyes, bulging from behind his bottle-bottom lenses. But his weird looks faded into the background once you knew him. He was playful, not like the other fathers, who just wanted to talk about work all the time. He even liked to play Twister, and Ouija board, and spent time with us kids when there were family social events.

"I couldn't believe it," Mom remarked on the way home from a party one evening. "All the adults were seated for dinner, except for Bill. 'Where is he?' we asked, and sure enough, he was rolling around on the floor with the dog. Geraldine begged him to act his age." Geraldine was Rose's mom, also well-loved in the community for her bright red hair and witty *joie de vivre*, as though Lucille Ball herself had landed in Abidjan. "But she told me she can't control him."

"It's a wonder he gets any work done," Dad said as we pulled into the long driveway of our home. The guard saluted us as we waved through the windows.

"This is a *maaahvelous* book," I said, in a hoity-toity British accent one afternoon at Rose's house. We were sitting at the dining room table drawing illustrations of Calamity Collision in action.

"Just splendid, *dahling*," Rose said. We both giggled, but then she became pensive, chewing on the cap of her magic marker. "How will we get it published?"

I shrugged. It had never occurred to me we'd have to figure that part out. In my mind, we were going to finish writing the book and the rest would take care of itself.

"I know!" Rose's face brightened. "We'll mail it to Judy Blume. She'll know what to do."

I wasn't convinced it would be that easy, but before I could say so, Mr. Mulcahy came into the room. "Hey gals, what's cookin'?"

Rose didn't look up from her drawing. "Don't bug us, Dad. We're working."

"Well, I'm working on my spare tire." He grabbed his doughy middle. "Hey, Fatso," he addressed me directly with the nickname he had given me, hilarious because I was stick skinny. He was always teasing me, but I liked it, liked being the center of attention. "You want me to make you some *pizillis*?"

Pizillis were donuts in Italian, or so he claimed, though as an adult, I would never find a single reference to them in any books on Italian cooking. But he made them every weekend, and even some afternoons after work, claiming the recipe as proof of some distant Italian heritage.

"Yes!" I dropped my pen and turned to Rose, still focused on her drawing. "Pizillis!"

Then she dropped her pen too, and we chanted. *"Pi-zi-llis! Pi-zi-llis!"*

"Coming right up!" He walked toward the kitchen, singing in a phony opera voice, while rumbling out a long and winding fart.

"Dad!" Rose shouted. "GROSS!"

She was embarrassed, but I laughed my head off. "Your dad is hilarious!"

We went back to coloring in silence. Then Rose said, "I wish my dad was like yours."

"*Why?*"

"Cause he's normal."

"What's so great about that?" My mind flashed to my father. He was so *stable. Reliable. A good provider.* These were things that Mom, who had grown up poor and without a father, always emphasized. But he wasn't *fun*, not like Mr. Mulcahy.

"Well, I bet he doesn't fart like that—"

"Oh, he does." I nodded for emphasis. "All the time."

"At least he doesn't make you go to Mass every Sunday. And those family walks? I wish my dad did stuff like that."

Dad liked to take long walks, and with my mother had been in the habit of an after-dinner stroll for as long as I could remember. Sometimes they made my sisters and me go with them. Rose had come along with us once, when she slept over at my house.

The route was always the same: left out the gate, down Rue de Hibiscus until the lookout point, where we could see the lagoon, a thick sludge of green sea water in the middle of Abidjan. On the way there, we passed the Ivoirian President Félix Houphet-Boigney's guesthouse. The Central African Republic's exiled president, Jean-Bedel Bokassa, notorious for his purported cannibalism, had been given asylum in the Ivory Coast and was staying there. Every time we walked past, I stole glances for a sight of him, as my mother cackled, "The better to eat you with, my dear!"

Rose had already gone back to Calamity Collision, but my mind was stalled on Bokassa. I imagined my dead body stretched out on the dining room table while he ate me with a spoon. Then I imagined him eating me *alive*. I felt sick with fear, even as I smelled the sweetness coming from the kitchen. Not even the crackling sound when Mr. Mulcahy dropped the dough in the oil and the shake of the sugar box when he coated the *pizillis*, cooling on the plate, could take away the feeling that a child-eating monster was going to get me.

CHAPTER THREE

USA, 2016

We touched down in Seattle in mid-June. It rained the morning we arrived, and everything was fresh, as though the city had spiffed itself up to greet us. This was the last place I lived in the United States as a single person, and I felt something both nostalgic and final inside me, seeing the city as bookends on my relationship with Tano. When I was last here, I hadn't even known he existed, and now I was back, without him, as if that whole life had never happened.

Except, of course, it had, and Carmen and Lorenzo were the proof.

They loved everything about Seattle; the outdoorsy vibe was not that different to Geneva, but the eclectic aesthetic of the people was new. "Did you see the piercings all over that guy's eyebrows?" Lorenzo said, thrill written all over his face. "The girls here dress so cool," Carmen remarked, every time we saw another unexpected outfit: plaid with stripes, vintage mini-dresses with thigh-high boots, Daisy Dukes with torn stockings. "It reminds me of London!"

"Seattle is awesome, Mom," they said. "Why did you ever leave?"

Grad school was the official reason, but it wasn't raw intellectual ambition driving the decision. I was twenty-five when I left, talking a big game—*I'm changing my life!*—driving off into the sunset, with my hair down and Evelyn Champagne King blasting from the speakers. I described that moment to the kids, in cinematic detail, as we stood in the driveway of the house I once lived in.

"Imagine my old, beat-up Mazda, packed with stuff."

"How much stuff?" Carmen said.

"Everything I owned." I remembered how it had felt to reduce the material contents of my life to what fit in the car. "You should have seen it; it was packed so full. And when I got behind the wheel to drive away, I realized the back window was blocked, so I had to dump stuff."

"But why did that matter?" Lorenzo asked.

"I wouldn't have been able to use the rearview mirror," I said. "And I had to see what was behind me." The kids laughed as I mimicked that former version of myself, frantically dumping things into boxes that got left on the steps of the home I was leaving. "It was hard, deciding on the spot what to get rid of, but I did it, and then I took off. All by myself."

"You were so brave," they said, starry-eyed, unaware that I was omitting the part of the story about being depressed and self-loathing. I wanted my kids to imagine me as the fun-loving Seattle girl who disco danced at the Timberline, sang karaoke at the bar on East Lake, went for coffee and the most wonderful hunks of cake at the Honey Bear Bakery. I didn't want them to know the flip side of that picture—how I had been desperate for men's attention, dressing provocatively, recklessly sleeping with pretty much anyone who showed interest in me. Though I was terrified of STDs, I never insisted on condoms, faking pleasure while praying to God the guy wasn't infected with anything. I hated myself for trading my health for affection, but set myself up, over and over, because I honestly believed it was the only means I had to inspire someone to fall in love with me. In my mind's eye, were that to happen, I would never have to worry about anything ever again.

And here I was. Some plan that had turned out to be.

Speeding down the interstate, buoyed by the kids' enthusiasm, under my breath I recited some encouraging little mantras to quell the angst.

You are strong! You are independent! Everything's gonna be OK!

I was actually starting to believe them until I got my first big fat reality check—*you're on your own, kid!*—somewhere on the Oregon coast. It was our first night camping, and nothing was going to plan. Erecting the tent was an ordeal that took hours, consuming the entire afternoon, despite the instruction manual's promise that it would be up in twenty minutes. Night was falling, and we didn't have any provisions—I had planned to go food shopping much earlier—so the three of us piled into the car and drove as fast as we could to the nearest Target, thankful that unlike in Europe, things never closed in the United States. As we charged up and down the aisles of the mega mart, my head was fuzzy with self-doubt: *Why had I thought camping was going to be easy?*

We bought a pack of firewood, the little fire starter bricks, and cans of soup and a bag of marshmallows that were going to be the evening meal. Then we piled back in the car and drove the fifteen miles back to our campsite, where I promptly realized we didn't have any pans or utensils. We didn't even have any matches to start the fire.

The campsite was sparsely populated, and I was already spooked, out there in the dark, though I didn't let the kids on to this. I'd seen some of our fellow campers earlier and though I didn't *really* feel unsafe, I didn't really feel safe either, with a group of six rowdy, beer-drinking men nearby. No way was I going to call attention to our presence by asking them for a lighter.

Lorenzo and Carmen tried rubbing sticks together, and I watched them enjoy the adventure, but inside I was irrationally furious at Tano for my oversight. *Where are you?* I cried inside my head. *Why aren't you with me?*

Suddenly, a camp attendant appeared. He was making the rounds, emptying garbage cans and getting ready to retire for the evening. When

I asked if he had any means to get our fire going, he rifled through his pockets and pulled out a matchbook—with one match in it.

I had one chance.

And I would not waste it. This fire wasn't just a fire, it was a symbol of all that blazed ahead if I stayed strong: a new life, a new me. And with that thought in mind, I threw all the fire starter bricks into the stack of wood, and said, "Kids, here goes!"

I lit the match.

At first, nothing happened. Then, as if by magic, there was a veritable bonfire, at least for the first minute, blazing as high as the flames that had brought me and Tano together. When the fire settled, the smoke made my eyes sting, and that wasn't the only problem: How to get the soup cans in the fire without burning our hands? I devised a way to toss them on the coals, but getting them out was another story entirely. They were boiling hot, the soup jumping from the cans into the flames.

I instructed the kids to roast as many marshmallows as they wanted while I came up with a plan for the soup. But I didn't come up with a plan. There would not be some magic way to save dinner, and so marshmallows it was, smashed between slices of bread with peanut butter. *Why not?* I tried to console myself, the cloying taste of marshmallow in my mouth. If this trip was to teach the kids about their maternal homeland, the all-American Fluffernutter seemed a relevant addition to the curriculum.

Then Lorenzo said, "I love the Great American Road Trip, Mom." Carmen leaned against me and put her head on my shoulder. "Thank you for bringing us to America, Mom," she said. "This is so fun."

Their words resurrected my confidence. I didn't know the future. I didn't fully understand the past. But this moment with my children was perfect, and I visualized the soup as all my fears, disappearing in the flames, like an effigy.

From Oregon we turned east—I was still too raw to go to California without Tano—and joined Route 50, otherwise known as "the loneliest road in America." We agreed its nickname was well earned; we were often the only ones on the highway for hours as we made our way through Nevada and Utah. The solitude was broken only by the biker gangs who started as small dots in the rearview mirror, until suddenly, as if by magic, they took shape, catching up to us, tattooed, leathered, unstoppable. The biggest thrill was the seconds we rode side by side, until they overtook us and disappeared, as if we were all on a runway to the skies.

Each time the bikers overtook us, I thought of a particular long-ago night in New Orleans, in the earliest days of my relationship with Tano. It was midnight sharp, on the way home from my waitressing shift at Fat Harry's Bar, when I saw him in the rearview mirror, running as fast as he could up Saint Charles Avenue. It wasn't the first time he'd had to chase me; he never told me in advance if he was going to meet me after work, and he was chronically late, so I never waited for him. But I was always happy to stop for him, to have someone to stop for … except not this evening. For whatever reason, that night it irritated me—his lateness, that he wouldn't plan ahead. So, I accelerated, pretending I didn't see him. What a radical act this seemed, refusing to stop! But he only ran faster, his arms and legs pumping like an Olympian in the rearview mirror.

In less than five minutes, I pulled over.

While the kids filmed the bikers flying by in all their glory, I was quietly consumed by this awful, regressive longing for Tano, acutely aware that now, every mile I drove left him further behind. But looking in the rearview mirror of my life, I was also understanding that twenty years on, I abandoned my marriage because twenty years earlier, I had abandoned myself.

In the early days of our relationship, when Tano would go on and on about the evil USA, how he was leaving and never coming back,

I would say, "But what about *me*? What am *I* supposed to do? I don't want to live so far away from my family!" But he was characteristically unbudging, and when I realized we were at cross-purposes—that my American nationality and culture did not fit with his leftist, revolutionary narrative—I stopped protesting and agreed: we would leave the USA permanently.

I remembered my mother's response when I told her about Tano's condition for our marriage. *"How can you marry someone and boycott their country? What does that say about him?"*

Now, as I started following the signs that would take us from the Loneliest Road in America to Bryce Canyon, I felt the heat rise in my face and realized that all these years, I had been asking myself the wrong question.

Who cared what it said about him?

I should have been asking what it said about *me*, that I would marry him anyway.

Somewhere in Arizona, a few days later, we checked into a Motel 6 for the night. We had done our camping duty for several nights in a row, and the hassle of getting the tent up and then down, coupled with the heat, helped me rapidly forget the strict budget I had put us on. And it wasn't like we were checking in to the lap of luxury. The rooms opened directly to the parking lot and a forlorn swimming pool in the shape of a kidney bean. I had visions of lying in the cool, air-conditioned room until the sun went down, but the kids wanted to swim. At first, I protested; dinky pools like that made swimming commensurate with rolling around in someone else's bath water. But it was a million degrees in the Arizona heat, so I changed out of my clothes and followed behind them.

As soon as we got there, I was engulfed by an uncomfortable feeling— nausea, dizziness—brought on by the smell of chlorine and the glare of the sun.

"Kids," I said, steadying myself on the guardrail. "I've changed my mind."

But they were already splashing around in the water and didn't pay any attention. Then I heard a voice. "Are you alright? Do you need help?" A tall man was crossing the deck toward me. "It can get hot out here."

"That's an understatement." I attempted to recuperate my wits. "It would be good to sit down."

"Join me," he said, gesturing to the rusted metal table with a parched umbrella emerging from its center, like a phoenix. "It's the only spot in the shade. I'll be right back."

I took a seat on the bleached-out plastic chair, and a minute later he reappeared with two cans of diet Coke and his iPad.

"Dennis," he said, extending his hand. I took the cold can—it was already sweating with condensation—and pressed it to my cheek, neck, and wrists. In the shade, I was better able to make out the details of this stranger who had come to my rescue. He was tall and fleshy, with an assortment of faded tattoos on his arms. But a once-sculpted frame was still clear, and that, plus his chiselled face, made for an unexpectedly handsome acquaintance.

While the kids swam, I chit-chatted with Dennis about his life on the road—he drove an eighteen-wheeler for a living—and our road trip.

"I can show you a bunch of shortcuts," he said, pulling up a map of the region. I nodded along pleasantly, only half listening, increasingly aware of his brawny arms. Already a fantasy was playing out in my mind: Dennis and I locked in an embrace on the orangey brown motel bedcover, his deep voice whispering his desire in my ear. It had been so long since I'd had any such impulse, and I felt embarrassed by my longing. *He probably isn't even attracted to you*, I thought, based on nothing other than the fact that I felt so unattractive. The sex had disappeared from my marriage years earlier. For a long time, I had felt invisible, disconnected from my body, as if it only existed if someone else was admiring it.

But the kids interrupted the vision; dusk was upon us and they were hungry. So, I thanked Dennis for the Coke and the tips and bade him farewell. I took a few steps and then looked back; he was watching me, and when our eyes met, he raised his diet Coke can, as if in tribute of something unconsummated. He smiled, dolefully—at least that's how I interpreted it—and I tried to convey with my eyes that I felt the same way.

As we drove to the nearby Denny's, I yearned to turn the car around and find Dennis again. It was ridiculous; we'd sat together for an hour and I knew almost nothing about him beyond the basic facts: fifty years old, from Arkansas, divorced, no children. Sixty minutes in this stranger's company, and now I ached for him? But something about his gaze had made me feel important, *seen*, for the first time in a very long time. Only much, much later, looking back on this moment, would I understand that I was less attracted to Dennis than I was to his desire for me; that the longing I felt was for relevance, and power.

As we ate, Carmen said, "That guy at the pool was hitting on you, Mom!" I wanted to say, *"What made you think that?"* I wanted to hear the whole story of what she had seen. If I would not live out this love affair, might I at least hear it narrated?

I never got to hear Carmen's observations because the waitress chose that moment to ask if we wanted more water, even though she had asked five minutes earlier, and the conversation was forgotten. But it had been enough to activate such craving that I had trouble falling asleep that night, desire heating my body like a furnace.

✳

Seven weeks and eighteen states later, the Great American Road Trip came to an end. When I turned in the key of our rental Jeep, we had covered 7,964 marvelous miles. The kids had been awed by the big cities, the small towns, the lakes and the canyons, the desert and the plains, the cowboys, the native Americans, the Harley Davidson riders, the hippies, the yuppies, the vernacular, the religion, the poverty, the wealth, the *size*. If their happiness was the only measurement, the trip had been an enormous success.

But from a literary perspective, *This Land Is Your Land* was no longer clear in my mind. Over the seven weeks, I had kept copious notes and tried to establish meaningful associations, but—niggling worry about money aside—now I was almost grateful I hadn't gotten the grant. Confusion had arrived instead of the brilliant conclusions I'd been so sure to draw. The story about discovering the United States had been eclipsed by memories of my journey, twenty years earlier, and the inner dislocation that had driven me into a marriage with someone whose relational conditions required me to erase part of myself.

And now I had much bigger worries to face than writing a new book. I had spent all my money on our trip; my account was down to a few dollars. I couldn't bear to tell Tano; I knew I would appear as an irresponsible child, and just as we were set to discuss our next steps.

A few days after we got back, Tano and I sat down to talk about our situation. As soon as he could secure a new place, Tano was going to move out. Because he traveled so much with work, we had agreed the kids' official residence would be with me, with no limitations at all on how much time they could spend with him. Carmen's plans for university in the UK were underway, so it was mostly Lorenzo we were thinking about in terms of the day to day.

"I have a financial obligation to you and the kids, which I intend to respect," he said. "But you'll need to look for a new apartment."

I just stared at him.

"Are you listening? You'll need to—"

"I can't move out of this apartment! What about my office?"

"You'll have to get something smaller. Less central, or maybe you can ..."

His voice faded into the background as my mind raced back over all of my offices past. Of course, I could get something smaller, less this, less that; I had done it many times before. But not now. Not at this moment where everything was up in the air and I was facing the greatest reinvention of my life.

"No," I said, quietly, at first. Then, as my answer registered on his face, I said it again, louder. "NO. I'm not moving out."

"We cannot afford two households if we don't give up this apartment!"

That Tano looked worried, not angry, sent my anxiety into overdrive. I was patently aware of how much money I would need to come up with every month to pay the rent and all the costs that came along with it. Even with his contribution, I would need to earn a hefty sum to cover my overhead. But this only reinforced my refusal. I needed this office as much as I needed oxygen and water at this point. Without it, I couldn't run my private practice, and then I'd *really* not be able to make rent, even if I found a cheaper place.

He looked me in the eye, as if he were about to argue. Before he could speak, I blurted, "I'll take on renters."

"*Renters?*"

"Yes, renters. Like a boarding house."

"Really." He said it like a statement, not a question.

"Yes, *really*. Do you have a problem with that?"

"Have you spoken to Lorenzo about it?"

"Not yet. But I will. And it will be OK. I know it."

"And if it's not, do you agree to move out?"

"*Obviously*. But it isn't going to be a problem. I know what I'm doing."

The irritation in my voice was a clever cover up. It was easier to snap at him—*I know what I'm doing!*—than to admit my uncertainty.

Did I know what I was doing?

I had to find out.

And if I didn't know what I was doing?

I'd bloody well figure it out.

I had to.

CHAPTER FOUR

Abidjan, Ivory Coast 1980

One weekend, after my regular Friday night sleepover with Rose, I went with the Mulcahys to the beach in Grand Bassam. It was half an hour from Abidjan, on a potholed two-lane road lined with vendors selling pineapples, papayas, mangos, and bananas. The fruit added a sweet fragrance to air that also reeked of smoked fish, an Ivoirian specialty. Most Sundays, my family made this same trip to spend the day at the beach hut we rented by the month. Dad paid for it with wads of cash and bottles of "special drink," Robitussin cough syrup from the Embassy commissary, coveted by the village chief. He was an older gentleman, with big, yellowed eyes, who would come by to chat. If he had been drinking, he would hold us captive with long speeches about how much he loved America. Dad would respond with his own speech about how much we loved the Ivory Coast. Sometimes, if there was any beer left in the cooler, they would drink a toast to the two countries. *Vive la Côte d'Ivoire! Vive les États-Unis!*

That was Sundays.

Today was Saturday, and I was with the Mulcahys at the Grand Bassam Resort. The resort offered the opposite experience from a day at our hut, where the ocean was wild and tar from offshore rigs littered the beach. Here, guards raked the sand clean and shooed away pesky vendors, who milled amongst the topless French women sunbathing on bright African cloths.

But we didn't come here for the beach. At the Grand Bassam Resort, the main attraction was the poolside restaurant, known for its delicious *steak frites*. The pool itself was long, rectangular, and overchlorinated; the water stung your eyes if you opened them while swimming. But a day pass at the resort meant as many towels as you wanted and easy access back and forth from the restaurant to the water.

We ordered lunch and went for a swim while we waited. Mrs. Mulcahy swam lazy laps, her red flyaway hair pinned in a bun with bobby pins. Still, long tendrils escaped, sticking to her face like a beard. She craned her neck to keep her face from getting wet, and her bright red lipstick and pale skin made her look like an exotic sea animal. Mr. Mulcahy played with me and Rose in the pool, throwing us through the air with such force that his wife scolded him. "Bill! You're going to throw out your back!"

He stuck his tongue out at her and winked at us, and I winked back, laughing. He hoisted Rose into the air, and she landed on the water with a smack, just as the waiters, young African men in bow ties and flip-flops, appeared, holding trays of plates under silver covers.

"All hands on deck," Mrs. Mulcahy called, already out of the water. Rose swam for the ladder, and I doggy paddled behind her, but as I did, Mr. Mulcahy grabbed my ankle.

"Let's take one last swim." He gestured for me to hop on his back. The *steak frites* were calling, but he was the king of the boat ride game, and it was a rare opportunity to be the only one in line. I climbed on, and he linked his arms behind his back to create a seat for me. Then he started to swim, legs only, like a frog.

We had done this dozens of times before, no biggie.

But this time, he slipped his hand inside the crotch of my swimsuit.

At first, I thought he didn't realize he'd put his hand in the wrong place. But then he started poking and pinching down there, and everything went weird, like a kaleidoscope turning behind my eyes. I could still see Mrs. Mulcahy drying her hair with a towel, and Rose shaking water off her skin. But I felt far away, spinning in a prism of shapes and colors, no longer part of this scene.

Mr. Mulcahy did the length of the pool, and then he stopped in the shallowest part of the deep end, where he could put his feet on the floor, and started jumping up and down in place. By now he had both hands in my swimsuit, and I was frozen, my eyes locked on Mrs. Mulcahy, who was standing at the edge of the pool, pointing to her watch.

And just like that, he pulled his hands out of my bathing suit. The elastic snapped back into place around my crotch as he let go of me. I wasn't sure what to do next, so I swam behind him to the edge. "Ladies first," he said, boosting me onto the ladder, kissing my back as I climbed out of the pool.

Sixty seconds later, we were all seated around the table, digging into our meals. Mr. Mulcahy cracked a joke. "You know why they call Kristin 'Crisco'? Cause she's got so much fat in the can."

We all laughed, but especially me. I bellowed with laughter, and the more I laughed, the more everyone else did, too. I was laughing so hard I wet my pants, so I ran to the bathroom, where the tile floor was covered with damp sandy footprints. I peed, squatting over the toilet bowl as I had been taught; if not, I might get dirty.

Dirty. Dirty. Dirty.

The word thrummed in my head as I stepped from the stall and stood in front of the mirror, de-silvered and cracked. I was wearing my favorite swimsuit, a red one piece with Snoopy embroidered on the chest panel. It was unravelling where I had picked at it, and I picked at it some more now, contemplating my image. I felt outside of myself, and oddly important, as though I had been chosen.

But for what?

What just happened?

My mind was all scrambled up. It was like knowing the lyrics to a song, but only inside my head; when I tried to sing them out loud, they disappeared. But it didn't really matter. I didn't need words, because I knew already I would never, ever speak of this. I would be way too embarrassed—of these references to my body, to the fact that part of me felt important for having been chosen. Besides, if I told, wouldn't it be treason? I imagined being outcaste, like the lepers around Cocody Marché, the stumps of their limbs wrapped in filthy rags.

We left Grand Bassam at the end of the afternoon and stopped for ice cream on the way home. I got a scoop of strawberry and it melted more quickly than I could eat it, trickles of red running down my hand.

"You're bleeding!" Rose said. "Call the ambulance!"

She had gotten a scoop of chocolate chip, and I eyed it. "I'm bleeding and your ice cream has poo in it."

We rolled with laughter while Mr. and Mrs. Mulcahy sat at the table next to ours, eating from cups; they had both gotten chocolate. I didn't think they were even listening, but suddenly Mr. Mulcahy said, "This is the best scoop of poo I have ever tasted."

There was a beat of silence and then we were all laughing, even Mrs. Mulcahy, who couldn't help but scold him. "Bill!"

"Should we get some more poo for the road?" Mr. Mulcahy stood up, wiping his mouth on a translucent, waxy napkin from the dispenser on the table. He missed a spot, making it look like a small moustache had sprouted in the middle of his lip.

"Yes!" Rose and I shouted, at the same time Mrs. Mulcahy said, "You're going to spoil their dinner, Bill." But he was already peering into the glass case that held all the flavors. Rose and I shoved the last bites of cone into our mouths and scurried to join him at the counter. I couldn't decide between mango sorbet or mint chip; while I contemplated my mind kept going back to the pool. But then it was my turn to order, so I pushed it out of my mind and said, "I'm just going to stick with strawberry."

*

A week later, it happened again, in the pool at the ambassador's residence.

And then again, in the pool at the Hotel Ivoire.

And again, in the car, when he drove me home after a sleepover. We were alone in the car —Rose was grounded because she hadn't done her homework—and Mr. Mulcahy kept his hand between my legs, gently rubbing as he drove, both of us staring straight ahead, not speaking. He only moved his hand to change gears, or when the beggar, whose eyeballs looked like they were floating in milk, came to the window shaking his cup, pleading for money.

Then it happened so frequently I lost count and I couldn't forget about it, no matter how hard I tried. It was like a TV show I couldn't turn off, but I figured out how to turn it down, and most days I went about my business with just a vague awareness of the hum in the background. The only time that didn't work was when it hurt, down there, because sometimes his fingernails were sharp. Then it stung when I peed. When that happened, I couldn't *not* think about it, and I felt angry, but mostly just confused.

Why did he want to do those things to *me*?

Sometimes I locked the door of my bedroom and stood naked in the mirror, studying my stupid, hairless body. I was the only dork around with no signs of puberty at all, nothing. The *only* girl in my class that didn't have boobs. No trace whatsoever.

No pubic hair.

No period.

Nothing.

Rose was so lucky, she already had all three, and when we were in the changing room together, and I watched her slip her boobs into the egg-shaped cups of her white cotton bra, I felt almost crazy with envy.

One afternoon, while getting changed for water ballet at the Hotel Ivoire, I just blurted it out. "What's it like, having boobs?"

"Like nothing," she said. "Like having a nose."

"*Really?*" I couldn't believe that. "A nose doesn't suddenly appear on your face."

She rolled her eyes. "Boobs don't just appear, either. You have time to get used to them."

I should have known this, because now my big sister also had boobs, and hers didn't show up overnight either. But I hadn't considered the getting used to it part. Maybe it was like getting used to her father touching me down there.

"Can we talk about something private?" Rose said, doing a quick scan of the room. For a split second I thought she had read my thoughts, and I had a flash of anguish, imagining losing her friendship. Surely, she would hate me if she knew.

Then she lowered her voice. "I wet my bed last night."

"*You did?*" That was the last thing I thought she was going to say.

"Don't tell anyone."

"I won't."

We locked glances in the mirror and then she added, "It used to happen a lot when I was younger."

"That's normal, for babies." I tried to sound consoling.

"No, but I mean like, even when I was big. Like *nine.*"

I didn't know what to say. That *was* a pretty big secret, but not as big as the secret that she and Steve Miko, the new guy one grade above us, had kissed behind the school last week at recess. And right in front of the bush with the snake that now looked like a blackened banana peel.

"I threw the sheets away. In the trash heap down the street from my house."

"Your mom is going to kill you!"

"She'll never know. She's obsessed with sheets. Every time we go to the States she buys, like, five new sets."

We went silent for a few moments as we gathered our clothes and shoved them into our pool bags. Then I said, "Why didn't you just tell her?"

"Because I don't want my dad to find out. He gets super angry about stuff like that."

"*Really?*" Mr. Mulcahy was always in a good mood. I couldn't fathom him angry.

Suddenly Ms. Nichols, the synchronized swimming teacher, was there. "Girls! What is taking you so long?"

We darted past her, shouting "Ready!" as she followed behind, clapping her hands in a call to action. "OK, people, take your places!"

The perfume of chlorine was heavy in the air. I threw my bag on a lounge chair and jumped in the water, an image of those pee-soaked sheets in my head. I could imagine them, in that ravine, where people burned their trash. Sometimes the wind carried the acrid fumes of melting plastic to Rose's house, and nothing, not even closing all the doors and windows, stopped the contaminated air from getting in.

I felt sorry for Rose, wetting the bed. But truthfully, deep down, I was happy. It made me feel less alone with that question that ached deep inside:

What's wrong with me?

CHAPTER FIVE

Geneva, Switzerland 2017

Tano moved out the weekend I was in London getting Carmen settled at university. When I got back to Geneva, the only signs of life were the cats, who followed me through the apartment, mewling, as if to warn me that something dramatic had happened. Lorenzo was with his father at the new apartment, just up the road, and I was grateful for my solitude as I went room to room, tears streaming down my face. I'd told Tano to take whatever he wanted, but he had left me almost everything. The one exception was the marital bedroom. Stepping into it, I lost my breath: it was empty, and I stood frozen, remembering the day we arrived in Geneva two years earlier and decided, together, where to place the bed.

I sat down on the floor and cried for a long time, accompanied by the shadows that beamed in through the window, like ghosts of a lifetime past. When I couldn't bear another moment of it, I crossed the hall to Carmen's room. It was exactly as when she lived here: stacks of books, half-drunk cups of tea, the imprint of her head on the pillow. We had spent time apart in her eighteen years, a week here or there when she went to summer camp, but never long, undefined periods, never a body of water between us. I clutched her pillow the way I had clutched her hours earlier at Heathrow, and then I collected the three—no, four— mugs, all stuffed with browning apple cores, and carried them to the kitchen.

Those apple cores had been my pet peeve for years. But all I could think about now was how much I'd miss seeing her lounging around the house, her long legs draped over the sofa, kitties on either side of her, reading a book, an apple core or two nearby. I already had a ticket to pop back over to see her in six weeks. London thankfully was only a one-hour flight from Geneva. But her absence was palpable, and more tears fell as I washed the mugs.

Carmen was my daughter, but psychologically I had been such a child myself when she was born that in many ways, I had grown up alongside her. I didn't realize this until I badly bungled an opportunity to protect her when she was twelve and targeted by a bully at her school in Paris. She begged me to let her handle it herself, but when the harassment persisted, I went into a crazed fury, telling the child off and then reporting her to the school, who suspended her immediately. I was triumphant: No one was gonna hurt *my* daughter!

Then the bully's mother came after me, and within seconds of hearing her scream over the phone, I crumpled in fear, literally shaking with this overwhelming sense that I was *bad*. I followed her orders to withdraw my complaint and request the school to rescind the suspension. Then the bully mercilessly enlisted all the other kids to reject Carmen.

I plunged into depression, ashamed of what I had done to my daughter and shocked by how easily I had collapsed in front of this raging adult. One of my closest friends at the time was a therapist, and it took one tearful conversation for her to point out that Carmen was the exact age I had been when my relationship with Mr. Mulcahy came to a head. "It's a regression," she said. "Something about the situation took you back to when you were that age and couldn't fight back."

That was the first time I saw my daughter's existence as fused with some buried part of my own, though the concept was still hazy. It would be many more years before I realized that deep inside me, a young girl was waiting for it to be safe to come out.

I put on the water for tea, and while I waited for it to boil, tried to avert the downward spiral of my mood. I cycled through all the common-sense action plans I made with my clients who struggled with mood swings: *Take a walk. Journal. Call a friend.*

I would not take a walk at this hour; it was nearing midnight. And I had never kept a journal, though I had always kept ideas. My shelves were filled with old notebooks, scrawled with plans and visions. Periodically, I would thumb through one of them and be amazed at how the thought I had once scribbled had actually turned into something concrete. My private practice had been born in one of those notebooks, as had my two memoirs, and the idea for the one I wanted to write now.

But what I really needed was a shoulder to cry on. I took my phone and tapped my best friend Olivia's number in my contact list. She answered on the second ring and whispered, "I'm not alone." Then she hung up.

I met Olivia in line at the grocery store shortly after we arrived in Geneva. She was striking, at almost six feet, with curly, rust-colored hair that hung halfway down her back. Originally from Ireland, she had been raised in Geneva by parents who worked at the United Nations. They had died in a plane crash years earlier, leaving Olivia a small fortune that she had used to buy a beautiful apartment when she left her marriage. We were the same age, and despite very different life circumstances (she didn't have any children and didn't work, having received a major payout when she divorced her rich, oil-trading ex), we had bonded immediately.

I'd forgotten that she had a date tonight with a guy she met on Tinder. I started typing out a message—*Sorry! Hope it's going well!*—when she called me back.

"That was quick."

"He's in the bathroom," Olivia whispered. "Just wanted to say I'll call you tomorrow!"

We giggled like co-conspirators and hung up, the surreptitious exchange jolting me out of my funk. I went back to the bookshelf and flipped through the notebook I had kept that summer, traveling back through all those American scenes: sharing a table with a group of mohawked vegans in Portland, the 4th of July marching band in Ely, Nevada; the herd of bison crossing the road in Wyoming; the Mormon carwash in Utah; the cornfields of rural Minnesota, where we visited my grand-mother's grave; camping at the Christian retreat in South Dakota; the busload of French tourists, incensed to discover that the hotel restaurant on the Navajo reservation near Monument Valley didn't serve alcohol.

It was time to make sense of this new reality, one that I had brought on myself by taking the kids on the Great American Road Trip, an adventure now forever conjoined with leaving my marriage. I booted up my laptop, envisioning that fun, zippy story I had planned to tell. My eyes bore holes in my notes, looking for a starting point.

But every reflection opened the chambers of my memory to reveal a different story, one that was much harder to write.

I couldn't tell the story of our voyage across the United States without talking about my marriage.

And I couldn't talk about my marriage without reflecting on my relationship with men.

And I couldn't write about men without writing about Mr. Mulcahy.

It was always back to Mulcahy, and now I was caught in a shadow dance; there was the story of *This Land Is Your Land*, and then there was the story behind the story. My mind jumped from one thing to the next, memories knocking into each other like dominos, falling so quickly I couldn't grasp a single one.

✳

Writer's block. Anxiety. Insomnia.

These were the reasons I booked an appointment with Dr. Daphne Invicta, a British psychoanalyst who had a reputation in Geneva as the therapist of therapists. Her schedule was full, but she agreed to fit me in for an early morning session. The day of our first meeting, afraid of being late, I raced out the door without breakfast and made it to her office just as fat, cold raindrops began splattering down around me. It was too early to ring the bell, so I ducked into a nearby café. My accent gave me away; after I ordered my coffee, the woman behind the bar gestured for me to take a seat, as she changed the tennis match playing on the large screen TV to CNN. I smiled, even though I didn't want to listen to the news, one depressing update after another.

Sipping my coffee, acid and hot, I pulled my notebook from my purse and jotted a few thoughts about what I wanted to cover in the session. There was the end of the marriage, obviously. And the kids, though so far, they both seemed OK: Carmen was adapting well to life in London, and Lorenzo to life divided between two apartments. Even Tano and I had settled into a friendly, albeit distant, new normal that didn't actually feel that different from when we still lived together. There was the worry about money, and taking on tenants, both of which were certainly contributing to the writer's block, and then there was—

"More allegations made against Larry Nassar, staff doctor for the US Olympic team, accused of sexual assault by dozens of gymnasts."

My stomach dropped at the breaking news alert. I knew vaguely of this Larry Nassar story, but I had tried to avoid it. It was getting press because Nassar was a doctor to high-level athletes, but I found it hard to believe he'd actually pay for his crimes. The world was full of Larry Nassars, abusive men who proceeded with impunity. They were a dime a dozen. I was so tired of this reality that seemed to never change. I tried to tune it out, but it was impossible to not listen; the reporter's voice was as omnipresent in the café as sexual assault was in the world. At the table next to me, a group of men played cards, and I had this irrational urge to confront them: Have *you* raped anyone?

Outside, thunder crashed, followed by a lightning bolt that illuminated the slick, wet concrete. My session didn't start for another fifteen minutes, but I had to get out of here. I stood up to leave.

"In a disturbing twist, we have just learned that gymnast Amanda Thomashow reported Nassar for assault in 2014, and that Michigan State buried the report."

What the hell? My heart was pounding so fast I felt dizzy. I sat back down and turned my attention to the television, as time peeled back to another place, pushing me there, pushing me to remember.

CHAPTER SIX

Abidjan, Ivory Coast 1980

Fifth grade ended, and our family flew back to the United States to visit my grandparents. They lived in Brockton, Massachusetts, in an elegant house they had built for themselves when my grandfather, a naval doctor, returned from World War II. The house was built on several acres of land, and at the far end of the backyard were blueberry bushes. My grandfather paid us kids fifty cents for every cup picked.

On the 4th of July, my grandmother served her customary non-alcoholic trifle, and the custard was stained blue by that afternoon's harvest. Everyone around the table was on seconds, except for me. I had barely started eating because I had been separating the fruit into distinct piles on my plate: blueberries, canned pineapple, green grapes, slices of banana. I performed this ritual at every meal, believing that if I divided the food and ate it in a certain order, whatever I was wishing for would come true. Years later, I would understand that this particular ritual was my attempt to exert control over my body because that control had been taken away from me. It was the first signs of what would eventually turn into a full-blown eating disorder.

But at the time, I exercised my new ritual with only one conscious wish in mind: *Boobs.*

Before each bite, I said a prayer.

Please God, give me boobs before my birthday.

I was one month short of my eleventh birthday, and the idea of going back to Abidjan still flat-chested filled me with anguish. Some nights I sobbed into my pillow, worrying about it. I couldn't sleep, the snores of my grandparents thundering through the house, so I read and re-read *my* autograph book, the one I got for Christmas. I had hardly been able to wait to pass it around on the last day of school, and since then, I had looked at the curly cursive of my classmates at least a hundred times: *2cute2b4gotten* and *CU at the end of summer!* and *It's been real,* a comment I didn't understand but pretended I did.

On the very last page, someone had written in black block letters: *Next year will you go out with me? Signed, your secret admirer.*

Rose and I analyzed it for hours, going down the list of the boys in our class. I had no clue who it could be. I didn't even have a clue who I should hope for it to be. When I was alone in bed at night, the air conditioner humming in the dark, thoughts about it rolled through my mind like waves. I imagined some faceless boy telling the entire class how he loved me, how wonderful and special I was. But then I remembered my stupid body. I didn't even have a training bra.

My wish didn't come true; I returned to Abidjan unchanged. A few days later, my parents dropped me at Rose's for a sleepover. We hadn't seen each other all summer, and she ran across the garden to pull me from the car.

"You are going to be so excited!" She jumped up and down. "I have the *best* thing to show you!" She took me by the hand and we went inside, straight to Meg's room. She pointed to the bed. "Sit. And close your eyes." I followed her instructions, and then she said, "Hold out your hands, and... open!"

In my hands was a green and white metal rod with the word CLAIROL written on it.

"It's a curling iron!" She clapped her hands. "We can feather our hair!"

It was better than a curling iron; it was the Clairol Crazy Curl, with steam! We got to work, and before long, we looked like the two girls from ABBA. Rose was the redhead, and I was the blond, though Rose's wavy hair cooperated better than mine, which was poker straight.

"And look," Rose said surreptitiously, sliding open the top drawer of the dresser. Inside were T-shirts, three neatly folded stacks, with cool things written on them, like *Virginia is for Lovers* and *If I Said You Had a Good Body Would You Hold It Against Me?*

The T-shirts hung just long enough on our torsos to cover our shorts, so it looked like we were wearing mini dresses. Then we took Meg's diary, hidden under the mattress, and locked ourselves in the bathroom. It was filled with details about kissing her boyfriend—what he said, what she said, where she put her hands, where he put his—*eeeewwww!*

Rose said, "Kiss me, baby," to her hand, puckering up and planting one loud smack after another on that soft space between thumb and pointer. The kiss with Steve Miko had made her kind of an expert, so I followed her lead, smothering my hand with my lips. It felt weird, and I cracked up extra loud to hide that it also felt kind of good.

"Come on," she said, after a few minutes, wiping her hand on her shorts. "Let's go listen to records."

Back in the living room, the needle of the stereo whispered—*get ready, get ready*—as it looked for the grooves in the vinyl. Then Samantha Sang's high, feathery voice spilled into the living room. We wailed along to her hit song "Emotion," slow dancing in each other's arms. Clutching each other and swaying to the music turned to fake sobbing, until we fell to the floor, pounding it with our fists, cackling at our hilarity. When the song was over, we played it again, but this time we sat side by side on the sofa, studying the album cover.

"Let's dress up as her for Halloween," Rose said. "We can put on eye shadow. And make halter tops." She pulled the hem of her shirt up and then down through the neck hole, holding it in place with her bra. I mimicked her gesture, but with nothing to tuck my T-shirt into, the knot wouldn't hold. As though she could tell just how much the absence of cleavage tormented me, Rose said, "Let's do more beauty stuff later." She pulled her T-shirt out of her bra and smoothed it over her stomach. "I'll ask my mom if we can make pancakes for a snack."

She ran down the hall to her parents' bedroom. A moment later, she was back. "My mom has a migraine. She said we can make the batter, but we have to wait for my dad to get home before we can turn on the burners."

Rose's words gave me a jolt; all the excitement about our reinvention into glamorous teenage beauty queens had left me with some temporary amnesia that Mr. Mulcahy even existed. For a moment, I had seen myself as someone that could be as powerful as the beautiful blonde from ABBA. Now that I remembered who I really was, I only felt self-conscious, with my boring hair and flat chest.

In the kitchen, we took turns cracking the eggs into the bowl and whisking them into the milk and flour. We couldn't melt the butter until Mr. Mulcahy got back, so when we had done everything we could without his help, we sat at the dining room table and worked on Calamity Collision. With the illustrations, it was now fifty-four pages long!

We were discussing whether it was ready to mail to Judy Blume when we heard the crunch of tires on gravel.

"Finally!" Rose ran to the heavy glass doors that took two hands to slide open. "Mom said we can make pancakes!" she called across the garden. "But we need you to light the stove for us."

The car door slammed, and Mr. Mulcahy and the guard exchanged greetings. I stood behind Rose as he approached the house.

"Look at that!" he said. "Fatso's back!"

"Can you help us?"

He mimicked me in a Minnie Mouse voice. *"Can you help us?"*

"Dad!" Rose said, pulling at his arm, and he said *"Dad!"* and pulled at hers. Then he said, "I'll turn the stove on, and you girls can start cooking while I change out of my work clothes."

"We still have to melt the butter," I said, following him into the kitchen, and he mimicked me again in that high-pitched voice.

"Hey! Stop imitating me!"

"Hay is for horses, also for cows. Pigs don't eat it 'cause they don't know how."

"You're so annoying, Dad," Rose said, as he lit the stove, and then, with a knife, slid the butter we had packed so carefully into the measuring cup, into the skillet.

"I wanted to do that!" Rose pouted. "No fair. I call first flip!"

"I call second!"

"And I call 'keep the flame on low or the butter will burn.' I'll be right back."

He walked away, singing in baritone, *"So come with me and we'll go and see the Big Rock Candy Mountains—"*

"Shut up!" Rose shouted. "Mom has a migraine!" but he had already disappeared into the back of the house. As we whisked the melted butter into the batter, we heard Rose's mom say, "Bill! Keep it down! *Please.*"

By the time Mr. Mulcahy came back to the kitchen, Rose had flipped six pancakes that were keeping warm under a tea towel. I had just poured my first two and was watching the little bubbles rise to the surface.

"Take this to your mother," he said, pouring a tall glass of the sweet tea he brewed by sunlight, in glass jars, with lots of lemon and sugar. He handed Rose the glass and a bottle of aspirin and she skipped off, calling over her shoulder, "Save some batter for me! I want to make more!"

As soon as Rose's footsteps disappeared down the hallway, Mr. Mulcahy came up behind me and stood so close I could feel the flab of his belly pressing into my back. I acted like he wasn't there, using the spatula to lift the edges of my pancakes. The undersides were brown, so I flipped them, and as I did, he reached his hands around to the front of my body and rubbed his fingers between my legs, over the fabric of my white jean shorts. His breathing went all short and thick, but he didn't say a word. I pressed the pancake hard on the skillet with the flat side of the spatula, wondering how much trouble I would get into if I got caught letting him do this to me. Then I heard Rose humming in the living room, the static of the speaker sending a crackling noise through the air. Mr. Mulcahy pulled his hand from between my legs and stepped away, as the sounds of ABBA's "Chiquitita" began to play.

I lifted a pancake onto the plate, but I did it too quickly and it fell to the floor. Mr Mulcahy grabbed my wrist and took the spatula from me, and as he did, he looked at me with those laughing eyes, like we were just joking around, same as always.

Then Rose was back in the kitchen, singing along to the music. She stopped short in front of the plate. "That's *all* you've made? What's taking so long?"

"Fatso's been muckin' up the pancakes," he said. I laughed and poured more batter into the skillet, but deep down I felt something like betrayal.

"Takes one to know one, Dad," Rose said, fishing another spatula from the drawer and using it to poke the soft roll of his belly. He swatted it away, so hard it flipped up and hit her in the face.

She burst into tears. "That hurt!"

"That hurt!" he mimicked, back to using his best falsetto. I stared at a splotch of batter on the floor. "Clean that up," he said. Rose was tearful as she took a paper towel to wipe away all traces of this moment.

"And get a new bottle of syrup from the pantry," Mr. Mulcahy said. "The good stuff, from Vermont. Bring me some when they're ready." He walked off, singing "Mairzy Doats," and Rose stepped into place next to me at the stove.

"Here," I said, handing her the spatula, not sure what else to do. "Want my turn?"

❋

The next morning, my parents called to say they were running twenty minutes late to pick me up for our beach excursion. Rose and I begged her parents to let her come with us instead of going to Mass. But they refused, so I agreed with my parents that I would wait for them inside the house; it wouldn't be long.

Then Mr. Mulcahy said that he didn't feel right leaving me all alone; he'd wait with me. I felt my stomach drop, and then drop again as I stood at the sliding glass door, watching Rose and her mom cross the garden to the driveway. I had never been alone with him, truly *alone*, not like being in a car with the whole world just outside the window. I understood that this was something different, and I was filled with trepidation, so acute that even now, years later, I can remember how it felt, the chill of the air conditioner making the skin on the back of my bare legs almost cold to the touch.

"Close the door, Fatso."

Mr. Mulcahy was standing in the doorway that divided the living from the bedroom area. He was dressed up for church, in an ornately embroidered shirt from the Philippines. The handiwork of the garment was beautiful, but the thin cotton strained against the bulge of his spare tire, and on him it didn't look elegant at all.

"You're letting in all the hot air," he said, taking a step toward me. His voice was greedy, his lower lip all wet and wobbly. "As a matter of fact, *you're* full of hot air."

I turned around to face him, pressing my body against the glass, cool and smooth on the backs of my thighs. Heat poured into the house. He took another step and held out his hand. "Come here."

The guard was talking to someone over the gate, and for an instant, I thought about going outside to sit with him. But things like that weren't supposed to happen, because I was an Embassy kid and he was a guard, and why would I sit outside in the heat when I was supposed to be waiting inside?

"Close the door," Mr. Mulcahy said again, taking the final strides to me. I was frozen in place as he pulled the door closed. I heard the lock click as he took me by the arm, leading me to the center of the living room.

"Give me a little kiss," he said, leaning forward, his drooly lips puckered. His breath smelled like toothpaste and something sour. I craned my face away from his, but his lips found my cheek.

I wiggled out of his grasp. "Gotta pee!" I ran down the hallway to the bathroom next to Rose's room. Inside, I turned the lock. I could hear his footsteps approaching, then his voice. "Open the door." I didn't answer, and he shook the handle. Then, silence. There was a small window with bars on it above the shower, and I could see the fronds of a palm tree just outside it. I heard the guard clearly, too, still chatting with someone in their dialect that sounded like fingernails clicking on a typewriter.

The handle rattled, and I jumped.

"I'm going to the bathroom!" This slipped out of my mouth and I felt instantly humiliated by this image I'd furnished of myself performing a bodily function.

Then I heard the honk of my parents' car, the sound of the guard's flip-flopped feet running to open the gate, my father's voice. *Bonjour!* I hesitated for a moment and threw open the door. Mr Mulcahy was not there; I didn't know where he was, and I ran through the house to the glass door. I struggled to pull it open, but I managed, and then I was out of the house, running barefoot across the garden, the soft squish of earth beneath my toes.

I felt like a robber making an escape, until Mom said, "Kristin, where are your shoes?"

"I can't find them," I answered, surprised by my own quick thinking. When had I become such a good liar?

My parents made that huffing noise that parents make. Dad turned off the ignition, and they got out of the car. My little sister was napping in the back seat, her head tilted back, mouth wide open. Mr. Mulcahy came to the door and began chatting with my parents across the lawn. I ran back up the stairs, past him, through the living room, down the hallway, past the bathroom, and into Rose's room, where my pajamas were in a pile on the floor next to my tennis shoes. I scooped up everything and took off back down the hallway.

Then I remembered my toothbrush, the new purple and green one I had brought back from the States. It was in Mr. and Mrs. Mulcahy's bathroom. Rose and I had gotten ready for bed there last night because we were playing beauty parlor with Mrs. Mulcahy's face cream and hair rollers.

I could still hear Mr. Mulcahy talking to my parents, so I crept into their dark bedroom, where the sheets and comforter were in a tangle on the bed, sunlight peeking through the patterned curtains as if to showcase them. I stood still for a moment, looking around, alone for the very first time in these chambers that smelled like sleep and newspapers. Months later, when the Mulcahy family was long gone, I would think of this scene. I would remember the tangled sheets, the hum of the air conditioner, the scent of toothpaste and shaving cream seeping from the bathroom into the bedroom.

Then I heard Mr. Mulcahy call my name. I snatched my toothbrush and ran out of their bedroom, straight into him.

"What's taking you so long?" he said, grabbing my arm. His eyes bulged from behind those thick lenses. "You're a good kid, Fatso." I held his gaze for a moment, relieved that he wasn't mad at me for running away. Then he loosened his grip, and I slid by him, his fingers brushing the bare skin of my legs as I did.

In the car, my parents discussed the menu for a function they'd be hosting later in the week. My little sister woke from her nap and played quietly with her Barbie. We picked up my big sister from a birthday sleepover party, and she came running to the car, calling out her last thank yous.

"Everyone buckled in?" Dad asked. Mom turned around to verify, and then we were on the road to Grand Bassam, like any other Sunday. I pressed my face against the window and closed my eyes. I was surrounded by my family, yet felt painfully alone. They had no idea about the secret I shared with Mr. Mulcahy, and the disgust I imagined they would feel if they knew burned a hole through my insides.

Over time, I became terrified people could tell, just by looking at me, that I was hiding something. I became animated, funny, *big*, to distract them from the truth about me. Shame, secrecy, cover up, coping. Every day that passed entrenched the paradox that was splitting my insides: hunger for attention conjoined with the need to hide.

CHAPTER SEVEN

Geneva, Switzerland 2017

When Dr. Invicta opened the door, the first thing I noticed was her age. From her voice on the phone, I had been expecting someone younger, but standing before me was a tall, slender woman with a long grey braid, old enough to be my mother. Maybe this was why I felt young, stepping into her office, as though I was leaving forty years on the other side of the threshold. The room was painted in soft yellow with pictures of calming nature scenes on the walls. In the far corner was an analyst's couch, and I imagined lying down on it to be tucked in, like a child.

But she gestured for me to take the chair clearly designated for her patients, tissues in easy reach in all directions. She picked up her notepad and waited for me to speak. My eyes lingered on her colorful beaded necklace, and then I consulted the list I had improvised in the café. When I spoke, however, I said, "Have you heard the Larry Nassar story?"

"Of course."

"What a creep." Fury rose again as I thought of all of those gymnasts he had abused, and how many might have been spared if Amanda

Thomashow had been treated with any importance. "It makes me so angry." My eyes smarted, and I pressed a tissue to my face. "Sorry."

"For?"

"For being so emotional." I blew my nose and laughed. "That sounds ridiculous, I know. I'm just used to being in that chair." I motioned to where Dr. Invicta was seated. "Not this one."

"What does it feel like?"

An image of Lorenzo at his third birthday party came to mind. He'd been so excited to blow out the candles, but when I put the cake in front of him and the room burst into song, he'd burst into tears. *Everyone's looking at me, Mom!*

"Like all the attention is on me."

"And?"

"I feel shy."

"Are you normally a shy person?"

"Not at all," I said, "Though sometimes that's just an act."

"Who's the audience?"

"Everyone?"

"Meaning?" She waited, pen poised, and I thought about all the ways I managed my social anxiety by making sure everyone else felt at ease, by being nice, and inquisitive, and funny. These were traits that had served me well, both socially and professionally, but I was aware there was a defensive aspect to them: keeping the attention on the other person meant I never had to reveal myself.

"It's hard to explain. 'Private' is probably a better word than 'shy.' I'm more private than people realize." I shifted the conversation to the writer's block, telling Dr. Invicta about my first two books. "They're memoirs, and they're pretty personal. I can't tell you how many people say 'I feel like I already know you!' because they've read my books." I laughed. "They have no idea how much *isn't* in those books."

"Such as?"

"Such as, I have a Larry Nassar story of my own." She raised her eyebrows, and I rushed through the headlines of Abidjan and Mr. Mulcahy, realizing as I did how long it had been since I'd repeated any of this. The story spilled from my lips as if in stanzas, like an old poem I'd been forced to memorize: I didn't even think about what the words meant anymore.

"Tell me more," Dr. Invicta said. "Start at the beginning."

"Maybe I should start at the end."

"Of?"

"My marriage." I told her about the choice I'd had to make twenty years earlier: leave the USA or lose Tano.

"Are you saying you regret it?"

"How could I? My kids came from it." I looked out the window; a pigeon was on the sill, looking in at us. "And I feel privileged to live in Europe. Every place has its problems, but I feel much safer here. I'm terrified of all the guns and shootings in the States. The issue isn't actually wanting to *move* there anymore. At one time, that's what I yearned for, because culturally, I *am* American. My family is there. And lots of friends." The pigeon flew away, and I turned back to Dr. Invicta. "So, no, it's not a question of regret; I've moved on from that. What I can't reconcile is that I didn't say no to him when it wasn't what I wanted. It never even crossed my mind to say no."

"Any idea why that is?"

I closed my eyes, focusing on the cascade of images behind my lids: younger me, arranging myself seductively before Tano, pulling out every stop to entice him: posture, expression, outfit, voice. I knew how to *be* wanted; standing up for what I wanted was much more complicated.

"That's what I want to understand. The simple answer is that I didn't want to lose him. I forgave anything to stay in his favor. The more complex answer is that the more critical he was of Americans, the more I wanted his approval."

"Can you elaborate?"

I picked at a loose thread on my sweater. "I spent a long time believing there was something intrinsically wrong with *me*. All the negative commentary about America and Americans just reinforced it." I laughed. "I *still* want his approval. God, that is pathetic."

"You don't show yourself much compassion."

"I'm a bloody therapist! Shouldn't I have resolved this a long time ago?"

Dr. Invicta smiled. "No one, therapists included, have everything figured out. Bringing hidden parts of ourselves to conscious awareness is a lifelong process."

Her words were comforting, and I would have said the exact thing to anyone struggling to connect the dots between their past and present. But it was impossible to show myself that same empathy.

"If I'm understanding correctly," Dr. Invicta continued, "it was more acceptable for you to sacrifice what you wanted than to leave the relationship. But I'm afraid we'll have to pick it up next time."

Sacrifice.

The word didn't sit easy with me. It inferred some sort of martyrdom, and though it had always been more convenient to blame Tano for being so rigid, I had to look at my role in what had happened as well. Could I really say I had sacrificed? Or just made a flawed bargain?

Therapy left me feeling weepy, but today there was no time for tears. Our first two tenants, recruited through an expat housing forum, were moving in that evening. Ursula, from Norway, was taking Carmen's room, and Agatha, from Holland, was taking the marital bedroom that had become Tano's until he moved out.

I lugged the vacuum from the hallway closet, turned it to max strength, and went to war with the cat hair and dust that had gathered since Tano and Carmen had left. The vacuum made a satisfying *whiiip* with every particle it inhaled, and as I bustled between rooms, I couldn't help but think about the fact that both girls arriving were twenty-six, the same age I had been when I met Tano.

I felt like a den mother, preparing for their arrival. When I was their age, I could have used a guardian angel. I desperately needed guidance, but the events in Abidjan had made me reticent to show any vulnerability to my parents. I was so afraid of worrying them, of appearing as anything other than perfectly fine, that I pushed them away, only letting them see the parts of me that were bright and shiny. That they had been far, far away until I was twenty-four—first in Indonesia, then Nigeria—in an age when long-distance calls were still prohibitively expensive and email didn't yet exist, had made it easy to maintain this emotional distance. When I did see them, we stuck to polite exchanges about current events and the weather.

I made up the beds in each girl's bedroom, using the new sheets I had bought for this moment, identical sets, crisp cotton, an egg-white backdrop decorated with delicate flowers, strawberries, and humming-birds. As I fluffed the pillows and arranged them just so on the bed, the front door slammed. Lorenzo's voice came down the hallway. "Mom?"

"In here!"

His face appeared in the doorway. "What are you doing?"

"Today's the day—"

"Oh God," he said. "*Renters?*"

I laughed. "Come on, we've talked about this."

"Can't Pop just move home so we don't have to deal with them?"

I looked at my darling son, with his wide blue eyes and rough-and-tumble hair. He was only twelve, but his voice had recently cracked. Puberty was fast approaching, but right now, he was still a kid. What was the right way to answer? An explanation of how things fall apart between adults? An explanation of our differences? An explanation that I was forty-seven going on twenty-seven, and the time had come for me to figure some things out?

The answer I settled on was, "No, honey, he can't. And we need the money."

"OK," he said, back to his usual lighthearted tone. "I'm going to the skate park." He skipped from the room and a second later, I heard the clatter of the peanut butter lid on the counter. I smiled, imagining my tall, reedy boy consuming thousands of calories that would barely stick to his growing frame. Then I went back to my room-fluffing, digging in the linen closet for matching towels, one set per girl, folded and placed at the foot of their beds, hotel style. This was actually kind of fun, and the more I thought about it, the more I liked the idea of being a strong female figure to these two young women coming to Geneva on their own. In some strange way, it felt like a *Sliding Doors* moment. Interacting with them would be a chance to go back in time, to experience a vicarious do-over, to see what it would be like to have made different choices.

CHAPTER EIGHT

Abidjan, Ivory Coast 1981

Finally! *Finally!* Boobs!

I had only the teeniest hint of them, but wore my training bra like a badge of honor (even though it was so uncomfortable I could hardly stand it). I still didn't have my period, but now I at least looked like a real girl, and I charged as fast as I could into my new femininity, under the tutelage of *Seventeen* magazine.

How to apply lip gloss that says Kiss Me!
Six styles that say I'm Smart—and Sassy!
Looks that will make heads turn!

Swimming and bowling at the Hotel Ivoire, once upon a time my most beloved after-school activities, were all but forgotten now that Rose and I had discovered boys. The hotel was the perfect place to practice the lessons of our teen magazines, on the spates of gorgeous Lebanese guys that hung out there, with their lingering eyes and slicked back hair. We dressed up in our miniskirts and ballerina flats and put lipstick on each other in the hotel bathroom, though we always lost courage and wiped it away before "casually" strolling through the hotel, arms linked, footsteps in coordinated unison. We dared each other to make eye contact with the guys we crossed paths with, crumpling with laughter when we did. We were *upside down and inside out,* just like Diana Ross, whose voice blared from the hotel record shop, where people thumbed through albums while shooting coy glances at each other.

One day, we spotted a group of cute guys sitting in the hotel ice cream parlor, their tall sundae glasses clouded with the last streaks of raspberry sauce and *crème Chantilly.* They were huddled together over a newspaper, laughing, high-fiving each other, as though they had just won a tournament.

Rose and I stood at the counter, pretending to study the list of flavors, discussing in low tones whether we should take the table next to theirs. But they got up and left, thwarting our plans. Rose pushed some money into my hand and said, "Get me an orange Fanta." Then she scooted to their abandoned spot. When I joined her a few minutes later, two Fantas in hand, she had this look on her face: *Jackpot!*

"Look," she said, her eyes shining. Underneath the table, she was clutching the newspaper. It was the *Daily Star,* a tabloid from England, folded open to a photo of a woman with huge boobs. She posed with her hands on her hips, topless, beaming at the camera, as though *she* were the one who had won the lottery.

"We can't let anyone see," Rose said, her voice conspiratorial. She shoved the newspaper under her shirt, and we erupted in giggles, getting hold of ourselves only long enough to chug back our sodas. Then we ran, contraband pressed to Rose's stomach, laughter pealing through the elegant corridor of the hotel, past the record store, the jewelry store, and the news shop where this treasure had likely been purchased. We made it to the nearest bathroom and locked ourselves in a stall, burping the Fanta for one last hilarious moment before getting down to business.

Perched together on the lid of the toilet seat, we kept our balance as best as we could as we smoothed the paper open on the bumpy terrain of our laps. We were silent as we examined the photo, fascinated at the sight of those big boobs and the headline, in bold, black print:

SHE'S THE BOSS.

Her name was Irene, and she was a twenty-six-year-old mother of two from Darbyshire who liked to keep her home spit-spot for her husband. He was the boss of his own company, the article said, and Irene was the boss of the house, the children, the cleaning, and the cooking. And she was a perfect double D.

"What does that mean?" I asked.

"Bra size," Rose said. "It means her boobs are so big she needs to get an extra-large over-the-shoulder-boulder-holder."

We went into another fit of giggles, thrilled to have a situation on our hands that merited that expression, imported from the United States by the big brother of one of our classmates. We sat there for a while longer, until Rose said, "Let's go look at albums." She stood up and unlocked the door of the stall.

"Wait! What do we do with *this*?" The newspaper felt hot in my scandalized hands, as if I, myself, had recruited Irene to take off her clothes for the camera.

"I can't keep it," Rose said. "My parents would ground me forever if they saw it."

I hesitated. I had no idea if my parents would ground me; this was unchartered territory. But I wasn't ready to stuff Irene in the bin with all those soggy paper towels, so I folded the paper as tight as I could and stuffed it under my shirt.

✳

When my parents picked us up later that day, it horrified them to see us standing in the middle of a group of guys.

"Sleazebags!" Mom gasped. "They must be twenty-five years old!"

"Eighteen," we said, in unison.

"They *say*. And even if that were true, they'd still be far too old for you girls."

"We forbid you to associate with them," Dad said in that stern tone.

I rarely talked back, but this time I was defiant, protective of our fun. "Why? What's wrong with them?"

"They could be dangerous!" Mom turned to look at me in the back seat. "They could molest you!" She shuddered. "Perverts!"

In the rearview mirror, I could see their frowning brows. Back at home, they went straight to the house, but Rose and I lagged in the garden. As soon as they were inside, we were in stitches again. *"Sleazebags! Perverts!"* We said the words over and over, bumping hips, arms slung around each other's shoulders. The power of our budding teenage selves fuelled us, and nothing they said could put a damper on that energy exploding from within.

That evening, when Rose had gone home, I locked my bedroom door and smoothed the newspaper open on the floor. I looked at the boobs for a very long time and felt something unidentifiable, some mix of taboo and longing. This was how women were supposed to be, unclothed and proud of it. Then I went to the front of the newspaper and started slowly turning the pages.

Prince Charles had just married Lady Diana. That took up four whole pages. France had performed a nuclear test, whatever that meant. The Jackson Five were on tour. A robber-rapist interrupted a dinner party.

My eyes were transfixed by the headline:

HE MADE ME WALK LIKE A FROG

Eight guests and their hostess had just finished dessert when a man walked through the front door. He was holding a pistol and made the guests tie each other's hands behind their backs until the only one left with free hands was the hostess. He ordered her to take off all of her clothes and walk like a frog in front of all her guests.

They averted their eyes, but he said if they didn't watch, he'd start shooting.

Then he forced everyone to watch while he fondled her genitals.

I read this story over and over, and even after I shoved the newspaper under my mattress, the words pounded behind my eyes. *Fondled genitals.* I brushed my teeth for a long time, five times with my right hand, five times with my left, trying to make it go away. But I kept losing count and having to start all over, until my mother knocked on the door and said, "What is taking you so long in there?"

I couldn't sleep. Shame engulfed me, as though it was me that had walked naked, like a frog, in front of all the guests. The thought of being exposed gripped me so vividly I trembled under the covers.

The worst thing was those words: FONDLED GENITALS. I wanted to rip them from my eyes, stamp on them, scream at the person who wrote something that sounded so disgusting. People shouldn't be allowed to use those words; *that's* what was perverted.

But no matter how I raged against that horrible journalist, something vague was coming into focus: Mr. Mulcahy was a genital fondler.

A person who fondled genitals.

Mr. Mulcahy fondled *my* genitals.

The reality exploded inside me, tiny and toxic, multiplying like the most virulent germ, ripping away that scrim in my mind that had somehow protected me from this shameful truth. Mr. Mulcahy was a child molester. And he molested *me.*

I couldn't make it stop, that filthy revelation; it was in my head, my chest, my stomach, my fists, clenched so tightly I could put them through a wall.

Mr. Mulcahy was a dirty old man.

Dirty. Dirty. Dirty.

It was unbearable. All at once, this concrete information was upon me, spotlighting two truths, one about him, the other about me. He was a child molester, and I was bad. Because I had known this, hadn't I? Why else was I afraid someone would find out?

Years later, as a young adult in therapy for the first time, I would learn how the mind compartmentalizes, that it isn't abnormal for a person to not fully "know" something that is too unbearable to process. I looked up to Mr. Mulcahy. Rose was the best friend I'd ever had. I had been mired in shame and confusion from the first time he molested me in the pool at Grand Bassam. Even so, I had never thought clearly and directly about *what* he was doing to me. When I was forced to consider that what he was doing was "fondling my genitals," everything and anything I still believed to be good about myself came crashing down.

Whenever Mr. Mulcahy came to the pool after that, I stayed out of the water, even when Rose begged me to swim. He didn't seem to notice, busy as he was chatting with the adults and giving them a much-coveted break from parenting duties by taking charge of their kids. *C'mon, kids! Let's play boat ride!*

One day, I was at the pool with some other friends. Rose wasn't there, but we were expecting her any minute. I was sharing a floating mattress with Fran, a girl in our class whose father also worked at the Embassy. Our torsos were on the raft while our legs dangled in the water, and we paddled lazily with our feet while we chatted about how bummed out she was: her family was just days away from leaving the Ivory Coast for Saudi Arabia. Her parents were getting the house packed up that very afternoon. Her dad had received his new assignment months earlier, so we had all known this would happen, but still, it was a strange and lonely feeling to be saying goodbye to a friend.

"You know what I'm gonna miss the most about living here?" Fran asked, staring dreamily into space. "Madame Corvez."

We bust out laughing. Madame Corvez was our French teacher, famous for her high heels, heavy eye shadow, and crabby temperament. Every kid at the International School had a Madame-Corvez-screamed-at-me-today story.

"Kristin! Fran!" Rose was jogging towards the pool, waving hello with one arm, her blue terry-cloth pool bag swinging in the other. Mr. Mulcahy was ten steps behind her in his red swimming trunks and a red T-shirt. The combination made his arms and legs look more pale than usual, absurdly, like white sticks.

"Yoohoo!" I shouted.

"I'm getting out," Fran said. "I didn't know that *he* was coming."

Something in her tone made my stomach lurch, but before I could even process that, she added, "Has he ever … *picked* … at your … you know …"

Everything went fuzzy for a moment; my face turned hot. "*Crotch?*"

We shrieked with laughter—*that word!*

"*Crotch-picker!*" we screamed, snorting and guffawing.

"What's so funny?" Rose shouted from the poolside, spreading her towel on a chaise -longue.

"Oh nothing," Fran said, "We're just being weird!" Then, in a low tone just to me she said, "We can't tell Rose that her dad is a crotch-picker."

This set us off into more gales of laughter, but only part of me was really there. The other part was absorbing the shock: *He did it to Fran, too?* I had this strange sense of betrayal, though at the time, I could not identify the feeling, which made it a hundred times worse. It would take many years for me to understand the complexity of an abused child's psychological state. It's not like I *wanted* Mr. Mulcahy to do all that stuff to me, but I had started to think of it as the proof of my … importance. My value. Wasn't that why he had singled me out? Because there was something about me that was wrongly right? Or was it rightly wrong? I didn't have the words to explain it, not even to myself; it was just something I understood innately about my position in the world.

Except I hadn't been singled out.

Mr. Mulcahy lowered himself into the water, and Fran paddled in the opposite direction. I let go of the raft and swam underwater alongside her. In the cool, muted tones beneath the surface, I felt stunned by the discovery of my ordinariness.

A few days later, Fran left Abidjan. We did not return to the conversation before her departure. I was shaken by the revelation, but quickly pushed it out of my mind. Things were changing, anyway, now that we were older. Rose and I more often convened at my house, because I lived so much closer to the Hotel Ivoire. Mr. Mulcahy dropped her off and picked her up, but I almost never interacted with him anymore. I was able to push Mr. Mulcahy out of my mind, or at least to the far corners of it where I could almost forget what I knew about him.

Until the afternoon when Rose and I took a picnic lunch to the ambassador's pool after school. We ate under the umbrellas, chatting about the new kids at school, debating which song on the *Guilty* album was the best. When we finished eating, Rose slathered oil on her pale skin and lay in the sun, her math book covering her face. I swam laps, because I thought I was fat and, according to *Seventeen*, if I wanted to have a great figure, I had to exercise.

The water was liquid glass, and I sliced through it with razor-sharp strokes, lost in my own thoughts: *"Woman in Love"* or *"What Kind of Fool?"* Suddenly the water shattered and sloshed, a tsunami rising over the edge of the pool.

"You're such a jerk, Dad!" Rose shouted, beads of water sliding over the oil of her skin. Mr. Mulcahy had arrived. He often came to the pool for his lunch hour, and he'd cannonballed into the water. She got up and pulled her lounge chair a safe distance away, the metal legs sounding stressed as they scraped across the tile.

I ignored him and continued to swim. Then he was behind me, grabbing at my feet, so I swam faster, but he caught me, his grip strong around my ankle. I kicked him off, but somehow the distance between us had shortened and I didn't just free my leg, I also kicked him in the upper arm, hard. He yelped and let go.

Mr. Mulcahy was sulking on a lounge chair when Mom arrived with her L.L.Bean tote and my little sister. He stood up to greet them, the waistband of his bathing shorts tied firmly around his bloated, pasty middle. He looked like an albino Weeble Wobble.

"Sharon," he whined, rubbing his arm and grimacing. "Kristin was roughhousing, and I got hurt."

"Oh dear, is it serious?"

"It's really sore. I may have to see a doctor."

"I'm so sorry," Mom said, all sympathy and graciousness. Then she turned to me. "Did you apologize?"

"No, she didn't," Mr. Mulcahy answered. "She was too self-absorbed to even notice."

I locked eyes with Mr. Mulcahy. His eyes bulged as big as I'd ever seen, and he looked forlorn, pathetic. I felt guilty seeing him standing there like that, rubbing his arm. But if he thought I was going to apologize to him, he could think again, that perv. But he had already turned away, waving *helloooo!* to the stream of kids coming across the lawn.

One weekend in January, there was a barbecue at the Marine House. The entire Embassy community had been invited to ring in the new year and introduce the new arrivals to post. Most of them were single adults, but there was also one new family, with a daughter who was roughly my age. Dire Straits blared from the biggest boom box I had ever seen; the moms swayed along in their strapless sundresses, while the dads, dressed in long shorts and short-sleeved shirts, passed around cans of beer. It was a beautiful, balmy day with clear blue skies, and the smell of hotdogs and hamburgers in the air.

A burly marine named Teddy shouted, "Who wants to play chicken? Last one in is a rotten egg!" He did a somersault into the pool. A wave of kids ran for the water. *"Me, me!"*

Rose and I didn't even have our bathing suits with us. No way would we take our clothes off in front of the marines. Plus, we were showing off our twin outfits. We were both wearing white shorts and red T-shirts, and had swapped one of her blue Dr. Scholl's for one of my white ones, and we looked very cool, even though I had to shove my foot into her sandal, and she had to tighten mine to keep it from falling off. We were not about to jump around in the pool like a bunch of juveniles. Not with the marines watching. No way.

Instead, we straddled the swings facing each other, discussing how immature the other kids were. Then Mom walked up with a woman I didn't know. "This is my daughter, Kristin, and this is Rose, who belongs to Geraldine and Bill."

"Oh yes, I see." The woman nodded. "Nice to meet both of you girls. I'm Mrs. Baxter, and *that*," she said, craning her head in every direction, "is my daughter, Jenny." She pointed at a skinny girl jumping rope on the tennis court. "She's going into sixth. Is she going to be in your grade?"

"We're in seventh," I said, stretching my legs out like wings, hoping our cool shoe combo would get some attention. There was a big difference between sixth and seventh, and I really didn't want this lady and my mother, who was the queen of this sort of setup, to force a new friendship on me.

But Mrs. Baxter was already flapping her arms. "Jenny! Jenny!"

Jenny skipped over to us, the mothers made their introductions, and then the three of us were left alone at the swing set. Jenny had just moved from the Philippines, and her fifth-grade teacher at the International School of Manila had once upon a time been Rose's second-grade teacher.

It was fun enough to listen to them talk about their old school, but man, Jenny was a *kid* compared to me and Rose. She hadn't even *started* developing. And she probably couldn't care less; she was literally telling Rose about her teddy bear collection, that's how babyish she was. I tried to signal Rose: *Let's get out of here!* But now she was telling Jenny about Calamity Collision!

I had not thought about that dumb book for at least six months, and I'd rather not be associated with something so childish. But Jenny was laughing, actually laughing, at all the binds Calamity got into: running into a wall when his hair covered his eyes, eating red hot chilli peppers because he thought they were candy, riding his bike sitting backward on the seat, because that's how he actually thought it was done.

It *was* a pretty good story, for kids, at least. And Rose was getting it confused.

"Calamity's nose gets stuck in the window because of his nose *hair*," I said. "Not his nose size."

She thought about it for a moment and then turned back to Jenny. "Oh yeah, she's right. He has this really long nose hair."

"Why doesn't he just cut it?" Jenny asked, and then I remembered: that's why we gave up on our stupid book. It was too difficult to explain things like that, because of course he should just cut his nose hair, or make other obvious modifications to solve all his other dilemmas. When we first started writing it, it didn't occur to us that the story was less hilarious when the solutions were so apparent, and we hadn't been able to come up with an explanation for why poor Calamity Collision didn't realize there *was* a way out of every single one of his predicaments.

Without waiting for an answer, Jenny said, "I'm going to get a hotdog. Bye!" And she pranced away on her skinny little legs, the kind that were so spindly it looked like they could break.

"We need to finish Calamity Collision," Rose said, looking all fired up. "Did you see how she was laughing? She thought it was hilarious!"

"But what about the nose hair? It's like we built the whole story on something that sounds unbelievable."

"It's a *story*. It doesn't have to be believable."

"Well, I think it does. Otherwise, Calamity just sounds like he's stupid. And if he's just plain old stupid, we shouldn't make fun of him."

Rose thought about it for a minute. "How about this? You think of three explanations and I'll think of three, and then we'll vote for the best one and finish writing the book."

I agreed it was a good idea, and a few minutes later, as I squirted ketchup all over my hotdog, I was actually getting excited about good old Calamity Collision again. *Move over, Judy Blume!*

But three days later, after school on a Wednesday, Rose called me, sobbing. "We're being transferred back to Washington. We're leaving on Sunday."

"*What?*" Foreign Service moves were planned with months of advance notice, so this made no sense at all. My heart pounded. Abidjan without Rose? It's not that I didn't have other friends at school; I did. But not a *best* friend.

"My dad's needed in Washington." She blew her nose. "Like a promotion or something. The ambassador was just here to tell him."

"The *ambassador?*" This was unheard of. In the three years we had been living in Abidjan, I had not once heard of the ambassador going to other people's houses. It would be like if Ronald Reagan showed up at your front door.

"How can they just *make* people move?" My voice had gone up an octave. "Can't your mom say no?"

"She asked for more time. She asked if we could wait until the end of the school year. But the ambassador told her that my dad was really, really, really *needed* in Washington."

"What about Calamity Collision?" I said, and then I was crying too. But the phone started making that weird, high-pitched sound that meant the line was about to fail, and before I could say anything more, it went dead.

CHAPTER NINE

Geneva, Switzerland 2017

My little fantasy about being Agatha and Ursula's protective den mother went up in smoke within minutes of their arrival. They were smart, confident, and totally in charge of themselves. Rather than having that vicarious do-over I'd fantasized about, I had a massive burst of retroactive regret. When I had moved to New Orleans at their age, I immediately got involved with Tano, dividing my attention between him and my graduate studies, in a ninety-ten ratio. These two, both new to Geneva, were enthusiastically plugging into different sporting and cultural activities, attending platonic meet-ups that they'd learned about over social media, defining *their* interests, cultivating *their* lives. They were dating, too, and *tee-hee'd* openly about their conquests, making it clear that they did not see boyfriends as badges of worth. Their identity came from within them, not from the fact that so-and-so wanted to go out with them.

Not wanting to come off as a control freak, I only established two firm rules: 1) that they use discretion when I was working (I had thought this was obvious, until Ursula wandered down the hallway in a towel one morning, just as I was greeting a client) and 2) that they be aware there was a child in the house if ever they brought guests home.

Whatever dread Lorenzo and I had about two strangers in our home was eased by the fact that neither of them was there much. It was an immense relief when I overheard Lorenzo tell his father, "It's not such a big deal to have them around." Carmen flew home from London one weekend shortly after they moved in, and her assessment also boosted my spirits about the whole arrangement.

"It really *is* like *Friends*," she said, referring to her favorite television show, as we sat alone in the living room after having shared a glass of wine at the kitchen table with the tenants.

"Uh, not really," I responded, *sotto voce*. "It's *friendly*, but we aren't *friends*."

"You sure seem like friends!"

"That glass of wine was an exception. I'm feeling festive because you're here." I pulled her into a hug. "Normally I keep a distance. It's the only way this arrangement will work. I wouldn't want to live with a friend at this stage in my life, and definitely not while Lorenzo is still at home. That wouldn't be fair."

"Calm down, Mom!" Carmen laughed. "It wasn't an accusation!"

I blushed, realizing I sounded defensive. But I was still getting used to this new life, and fluctuated between relief that it was going well and awareness that I needed to keep strict boundaries at all times in order for it to continue this way. Friendly, but not friends. And it wasn't just to protect Lorenzo. It was to protect me. I was extremely busy, and the last thing I wanted was to socialize while at home. My days started at 5:00 a.m. when my eyes popped open. No matter how tired I was, I just couldn't sleep any later, a function of menopause and anxiety. So I'd get up in the quiet, put on the coffee, feed the kitties, and then turn on my computer. In that hour between waking and having to wake Lorenzo for school, I worked on my manuscript.

Dr. Invicta deserved credit for the fact I was writing at all. We'd only had a handful of sessions, but that had been enough to clear up the writer's block. "It seems to me," she'd said, "you're blocked because you're not allowing yourself to write the story you actually want to tell."

"But I *do* want to write *This Land Is Your Land*," I'd insisted.

"So, write it. But write the other story, too."

It was such a simple analysis, but it was the permission I needed to open a new document, still untitled, and transcribe what happened in Abidjan thirty-five years earlier. It wasn't a coherent narrative; it was a brain dump of specific memories I had never shared.

"Someone made an accusation." Your father stares into his glass.

"A serious accusation," your mother adds.

The room tilts, and your heart thumps in your chest, so loud you can hear it. You lean against the arm of the sofa. Outside cicadas sing.

I hadn't told Dr. Invicta that I was writing in the second person voice, using "you" in place of "I" to tell my story. I knew it was unusual, though not unheard of: I had read other books written in that voice—Jay McInerney's novel *Bright Lights, Big City* and Laura Fraser's memoir *An Italian Affair*—and loved them. And some of my clients, usually men, spoke in second person when revealing difficult information.

"You never think your wife is going to cheat on you."

"You don't go to work on Monday morning expecting to be fired."

It was much harder to speak directly about oneself: replacing "I" with "you" provided some distance from the pain, some universality. When my clients lapsed into second person, I often had them restate what they said using "I."

"I never thought my wife would cheat on me."

"I never thought I was going to be fired."

Making that "simple" shift was usually all it took for the emotion to flood to the surface. The fact that I was doing the same thing in my writing wasn't a conscious decision; something alchemical was at play, this detached voice allowing a new tenderness for myself to grow where there had once only been shame. It would still take some time for me to recognize this outcome, though the theme of detachment was something I had already been discussing with Dr. Invicta as I continued to process my new "head of household" status.

"It hits me sometimes," I said to her one day, "that by having Tano in charge of all the finances, I was also relying on him to be in charge of *me*." I shook my head in disbelief. "I think I turned him into a father figure."

I thought of the queasy feeling I got every time I saw an official-looking envelope in the mailbox, how I held my breath every time I opened a bill, terrified I wouldn't have enough money to pay it. Tano had protected me from all of that, simply by being in charge. I felt sheepish, *stupid*, for being so disconnected. In all the years together, I could not think of a single time that *he* got any bad financial surprises: he knew exactly what needed to be paid and when, and he had money set aside to cover it all. He was like my dad, who had also protected us from ever having to think about that stuff.

"But I'm changing." Over the years, I had become so locked inside my resentment at Tano's anxious control of our money that I had overlooked the value in his austerity. Now I paid attention to how much money I had in my wallet and thought twice before whipping out my credit card (the shared AmEx was gone) to buy whatever I wanted. I had never dropped large quantities of money on expensive handbags or fancy clothes. My casual attitude about spending was reflected more in going out to eat whenever I felt like it, or getting a massage, a pedicure, a treat in a café. Not anymore.

Dr. Invicta nodded. "I'm impressed with your efforts." She knew that I was saving as much as I could to start a retirement fund, while still having enough money for periodic visits to London to see Carmen.

"Thanks. And to be honest, I'm impressed too. I was so scared a few months ago, and now I realize that I am totally capable of managing my life."

Dr. Invicta clapped, and I took a mini bow from my chair. "I've been wanting to show you this," I said, digging in my purse for the brochure of a workshop that would take place in the French countryside in the spring. Organized by a European writer's association, it featured a prolific English novelist, Alistair Grand. "Eventually, I'd like to sign up for something like this."

Dr. Invicta skimmed the paper. "I think that's a wonderful idea!"

"I've read four of Alistair Grand's novels. I even heard him speak many years ago, during my college days when he was on tour in the United States." I hesitated. "It's pretty expensive, though."

"It would be an investment in yourself. Have you ever attended something like this before?"

My mind flashed back to a few years earlier when I was writing my first book, *Trailing*. I had applied for a writer's retreat that took place every year on the Amalfi Coast. It was expensive enough that had I actually expected to be offered a spot, I wouldn't have even applied. When the offer came in, I stressed over it for two days and then turned it down after Tano said, "Why would you spend all that money if your objective is to write a book? Why wouldn't you just stay home, for free, and *write?*"

I remember how disappointed I felt in that moment. What I yearned for him to say was, *That's wonderful, darling! I'm so proud of you! Pack your bags! I'll stay with the kids!* At the same time, I knew we had little disposable income and felt ashamed for even considering it as something I might do. Fancy retreats were in the same category as business class flight tickets—only for other people.

"No," I said. "And I still don't know if I'll sign up for this one because of the money. But I'll have to decide soon. The deadline is in a month."

"Is it only the money that's giving you pause?"

"It's mostly the money." I shifted in my chair. "But if I'm honest, it's also fear. To apply, you have to submit pages of a work in progress. To *Alistair Grand*. I'm intimidated! What if he thinks it's …" My voice drifted off as I remembered showing the original draft of *Trailing*, in which I had included a few paragraphs about the influence of the Mulcahy story on my life, to a literary agent. He was a tough-talking Long Islander whom I'd disliked from the get-go, but he was the only one who had responded to the handful of query letters I'd mailed out. His reaction was brutal. "Take that out," he said. "My *Gawd*. No one wants to read another 'woe is me, I got groped' story. So many women have had much worse things happen to them."

I cut the passage. His reaction confirmed something I had been struggling with since Abidjan: that what happened to me really wasn't such a big deal. That I should be ashamed I'd let it direct so much of my life.

"What if he thinks it's what?"

"I don't know … not worth telling?"

"Not worth telling?" Dr. Invicta sounded incredulous.

But even as I spoke, I realized this belief was passé. I knew my story was important, and any doubts about that had been erased by the #MeToo movement and all the stories that were now being told, the secret pain of millions of women finally getting the attention they deserved.

I responded by saying, "Could I bring some pages to our sessions?"

She looked surprised that I even asked. "It goes without saying. You can bring whatever you like to our sessions."

I thought I would need a few weeks to muster the courage to share some pages with Dr. Invicta. But that night I read the *New York Times*, whose pages were filled with updates on the cases against Larry Nasser, Dominique Strauss Kahn, Harvey Weinstein, Bill Cosby, and Donald Trump. By the time I went to bed, I had so much rage in my blood I could not fall asleep. I wanted to *do* something; I needed a punching bag, or better still, a map to Larry Nasser's house. I would kick him in the balls so hard he wouldn't ever walk again.

But I had another outlet, one that was far more powerful than a kick in the crotch.

The words poured out of me the following morning, and every morning after that. The night before my next session, I printed some pages. I hadn't told Dr. Invicta the details of what had happened all those years ago in West Africa; it was too discomfiting to speak about. But I could read it to her, and the pages burned in my hand as I anticipated sharing them.

CHAPTER TEN

Abidjan, Ivory Coast 1982

The three days leading up to Rose's sudden departure come to you now as a sequence of images, as though from a movie, about a family plunging into crisis.

You and Rose in your living room, listening to "What Kind of Fool" on repeat, sobbing over the orders from Washington, "tearing you apart, leaving you pain and sorrow."

Your parents waving from the window of the Peugeot as they head off to Rose's house to help her parents pack out.

Sitting around the table at Edith Lippman's house, a huge pot of spaghetti and meatballs on the red-checked tablecloth, the last community supper with the Mulcahys before they leave.

A convoy of Embassy cars in single file on the road to the airport, filled with families who want to see the Mulcahys off in person.

At the airport, bottles of champagne. Speeches and toasts. Someone breaking into song. For he's a jolly good fellow!

You and Rose making your final promises to each other: you'll write every week, you'll meet every summer, you'll always be friends.

Then you stand with all the adults and kids, watching the Mulcahys walk across the tarmac to the airplane. Mr. Mulcahy keeps turning around to blow kisses, and some people in your group blow them back. Then he makes some gestures with his hands, something you don't understand but the adults find funny. They all laugh, and someone says, "Abidjan just won't be the same without Bill."

Rose and her mom are ahead of Mr. Mulcahy, and you can tell by the shake of their shoulders they are crying. Before they climb the stairs to the plane, they turn and wave. That is the last sight of Rose you will ever have.

That evening, your parents tell you that the new girl, Jenny Baxter, told her parents, on the way home from the Marine House barbecue, that Mr. Mulcahy had put his hand in her bathing suit. It was obviously a terrible misunderstanding, they say. You're as shocked as they are, no? Because certainly, you knew nothing about this?

You know they are asking rhetorically, that never in a million years do they imagine their twelve-and-a-half-year-old daughter will say yes. A split second later, you have destroyed your parents' reality. Everything they believe they know goes up in smoke. Friendship? Trust? Faith in fellow man? Gone.

You recite two years' worth of stories of being molested, not by the Lebanese guys they had forbidden you from seeing, but by someone they had trusted completely. The more you reveal, the more distraught they become. The more distraught they become, the more you speak about it as though it was no big whoop, just something you had been getting through, the way you got through homework. Something unpleasant that had become a normal part of your life. Something you had accepted.

The fallout from your revelation is more traumatic than the secret you have been sitting on.

There is your mother crying, "We need to call someone! We need someone to help us!"

There is your father standing at the phone, pounding the receiver button, listening for a dial tone. "It doesn't work, God dammit!"

There is the houseboy, Emmanuel, running into the room, wringing his hands. "Qu'est-ce qui se passe, Monsieur?" He looks scared, and your father tells him that le papa of Rose, whose goodbye party he worked last night to earn overtime pay, has raped you with his finger.

Emmanuel looks stricken and leaves the room; you feel you will suffocate. Why did he say rape? And are those tears? You have never seen your father cry, and it terrifies you. Then you hear voices coming in through the kitchen door. Emmanuel has run to get the Larsens, the next-door neighbors, also Embassy people. Mrs. Larsen hugs your mother; Mr. Larsen runs back to his house and returns, a moment later, with a shortwave radio. He sets it up at the dining room table, and he and your father sit, and make contact in loud voices, with whom you don't know.

You have no idea what is happening.

No idea at all.

Then, in the movie, the camera narrows focus, and the crackling of the radio, the loud voices, the crying all fade to silence. There you are, sitting in the gold velour chair. The shot closes in on you, alone. And then the camera plays the strangest trick: it makes you bigger, much bigger, at the same time you get smaller, and smaller, and smaller.

CHAPTER ELEVEN

Geneva, Switzerland 2017

Dr. Invicta kept her eyes closed as I read. When I was done, she opened them and said, "I'm very moved."

"You are?" I leaned forward in my seat.

"The story is hard to hear. I'm shaken by it." She poured herself a glass of water, but instead of drinking it, she set it back on the table and played with the colorful beaded necklace she always had around her neck. "And I'm intrigued by your use of the second person. Did you write your other books in that voice?"

"No," I said. "I've never written in second person before this."

"Is it a stylistic choice?"

"No." I glanced at the pages, crumpled by my grip. "Does it bother you?"

Dr. Invicta shook her head. "Not at all. But it stands out. It comes across as … dissociative … as if you're talking about someone other than yourself. Do you see what I mean?"

I knew exactly what she meant.

"It makes perfect sense," Dr. Invicta continued. "It's as though you have two voices, which is normal for anyone who has experienced trauma. The 'true' self goes into hiding, and the 'false' one steps in. When I listened to you read, I was thinking that it was your false self, narrating what happened."

"Yes," I said slowly, loosening my hold on the paper, placing it on the table in front of me. "That's it. But I don't like using that word 'false.' 'True' is all right, but 'false'? I think it's misleading. Out of context, it could be understood as acting fake."

Dr. Invicta smiled. "I've often thought the same thing. Too bad we can't get in touch with Winnicott and ask him to adapt the language."

I smiled too. Donald Winnicott was a British psychoanalyst who first described the concept of true and false selves. He postulated that the false self develops as a protection mechanism for the authentic and spontaneous true self, not yet damaged by all the things that can harm a person over the course of their childhood. A false self doesn't need extreme adversity or trauma to develop. It's inevitable that a baby, who comes into the world in a completely authentic "true" state, will develop defenses in reaction to the frustrations and disappointments they are forced to endure when their caregiver isn't attuned to what they need.

"What word do you prefer?" Dr. Invicta asked.

I thought about it for a moment. "I like the idea of true self, but I would rather call the part that develops in response to trauma the 'defensive' self. It's just semantics, I know, but it matters to me."

Dr. Invicta picked up her notepad. "Let's go back to your writing. In the piece you just read, it's your defensive self describing the experience of your true self, who 'gets smaller, and smaller, and smaller.'"

Hearing my own words played back brought a rush of feeling to the surface, and I dabbed at my eyes with a tissue. "I remember watching that girl get smaller."

"*That* girl." Dr. Invicta's words took up space in the room, and we sat in silence for a few moments as they landed. Then she said, "That girl got smaller and smaller while the adults went to pieces. And the girl narrating the story, she adapted. Can you read the passage aloud again?"

I picked up the pages, but as I opened my mouth to read, Dr. Invicta did the very thing I sometimes did with my clients. "Can you put it in *I* terms?"

I read, tentatively, as though I was translating. *"I speak about it as though it was no big whoop, just something I had been getting through, the way I got through homework. Something unpleasant that had become a normal part of my life. Something I had accepted."*

"You tried to normalize it for your parents."

"Yes. Everything blew up so fast. It scared me how upset they were. How upset everyone was that night. The houseboy, the neighbors, *everyone.* I just wanted to make it stop."

Dr. Invicta glanced at the clock. "We've gone over time. But before we part ways, I'd like to put another word on the table. *Adaptive.*"

She watched my face for a moment, as though she expected a reaction, but when I said nothing, she continued. "True self/false self. True self/ defensive self. True self/adaptive self. We can interchange these terms; as you said, it's just semantics. But I think it will help our process if we can be as precise as possible about what you were going through as a child. And I think the most accurate term is *adapting,*" Dr. Invicta said. "You were adapting. It's what children do when they have no other choice. They adapt to their situation."

I nodded, some new self-awareness clicking into place. I couldn't yet define it, but I was understanding, at a visceral level, the thick defense built into my psyche. My demeanor was calm, but inside I felt my blood pulsing, strong and anticipating. I didn't know what she was going to say next, but what she said already, what we talked about together, was revelatory in a way that felt big, as though I was on the cusp of something important.

CHAPTER TWELVE

Abidjan, Ivory Coast 1982

In the days after the Mulcahys' departure, seven girls between the ages of six and twelve, all daughters of US diplomats, revealed that Mr. Mulcahy did it to them, too. While the adults reeled in this stunning revelation, that the beloved Bill Mulcahy—*such a hoot, so generous*—was a rampant pedophile, I was reeling from the humiliation that everyone was thinking about *what* he had done to us, shining a spotlight on that most shameful part of our bodies. It had been disorienting enough to learn that Fran was also one of the chosen ones, but the discovery that he had "fondled the genitals" of so many of us was so overwhelming I didn't know what to do. I felt like I was drowning, but there was nothing to grab on to, because everyone was *devastated* by this *devastating* news which had left the entire community in a state of *devastation*.

I heard these words repeated, over and over, by my parents, and all the parents, who gathered at our house for an emergency meeting.

"How could this have happened?" my mother cried. I was listening from the top of the stairs, and I squinched my eyes shut every time she spoke. "How could we have missed all these clues? It seems so obvious now."

But in the early 1980s, was it so obvious? It wasn't common knowledge, the way it was now, that pedophiles are rarely strangers in the public bathroom, but known and trusted adults, who groom not just children, but entire communities, with their loveliness, their affection.

"Why do you think Jenny dared speak up?" another mother cried. "I am just *devastated* that our daughters didn't feel they could."

My parents had asked me the same question, and I hadn't been able to answer for the same reason I hadn't told them: it was too humiliating.

"She knew nothing about Mulcahy. *We* knew nothing about him," Jenny's father said. "The day of the barbecue was our eighth day at Post. Maybe if we'd been here longer, we would have also been fooled."

"She's a hero for telling on that bastard," another parent said. "I still can't believe the Embassy didn't tell *us*."

The following day, my parents made the same objection, in a meeting with the State Department psychiatrist who had been flown in to help. His name was Dr. Feare, though there was nothing scary about him, with his mild manner and soft Southern accent.

"We want to know why the Embassy didn't disclose the allegation against Mulcahy until he was on the airplane," Dad said. "All we were told was that there had been an unfortunate 'misunderstanding.' That Jenny Baxter 'misinterpreted' Mulcahy's roughhousing. We helped that monster pack up his house! We brought champagne to the airport! We gave him access to our children until the very last moment! Why did no one tell us?"

Devastated. Devastating. Devastation.

"There's no protocol for something like this," Dr. Feare said. "It's quite unprecedented. From what I understand, Washington didn't provide clear instructions to the security office here in Abidjan, other than that Mulcahy's civil liberties had to be protected."

"What about our civil liberties? What about the children's?"

"I'm so sorry. You have every right to be upset. But the handling of the case is really not my domain. I'm just here to support the victims." He turned to me. "Is there anything you'd like to tell me?"

Tell *him* something? I could barely look at him. The only one I wanted to talk to was Rose. I didn't want to talk to this strange man, or all the other victims, or my parents, whom I had never seen so distressed. *Rose* was the one I wanted to talk to. But I had no idea how to reach her. Back in Washington, the Mulcahys would stay in some State Department rental while they looked for a place to live. Rose was supposed to write first, with an address, but all mail came through the Embassy pouch, so the letters would be intercepted by my parents who had forbidden me to speak to her ever again. I wondered if she even knew what had happened, and I wondered how I was supposed to erase her from my memory, as if she had never existed.

Washington ordered an investigation to be carried out by Mr. Hornsby, whose son I regularly babysat. I wanted to die, truly *die*, when he came to our house late one afternoon, not to pick me up for an evening of babysitting, but to sit in our living room with his spiral notebook and pen. He wanted to have a "conversation." This conversation included many questions about my relationship to the entire Mulcahy family, as if they were all under examination.

Then he asked, "How deep inside your vagina did Mr. Mulcahy insert his finger?"

The air got heavy; it clogged my lungs and blocked my voice. I looked at the floor.

Mom was standing by the garden doors, clasping and unclasping her hands. "She's twelve! She doesn't know! How can she know that?"

Mr. Hornsby cleared his throat. "How about you show me here?" He pointed to his arm, where the blue cotton of his short sleeve dress shirt met his freckled flesh. I stole a glance at his face: bright red, beads of sweat on his forehead. "You can put your finger up my sleeve."

"Does she *have* to do that?" Mom said.

But I had already stood up, and Mr. Hornsby had, too, turning his torso to offer me his arm. I stuck my finger in his sleeve, and then yanked it out, like it was an electric socket. He wrote something in his notebook, and I went outside to whack a tennis ball, shame burning my insides like acid.

✳

"What is happening with the investigation?" I overheard Dad say one evening, weeks after the Mulcahys' departure. I was listening at the top of the stairs while he was on the phone with Mr. Hornsby, whose voice came through the receiver in staticky fragments.

"*Slow … very difficult … policies …* "

"Can we assume they will eventually lock him up?"

"*Laws … foreign territory … stateside …* "

"It's already a slap in the face that he hasn't even lost his job. That they have put him on the Africa desk adds insult to injury," Dad said. "Tell Washington it's bad for morale that those of us affected still have to work with that bastard! I still get cables from him. As though nothing ever happened!"

"*Soon … Washington … patience …* "

They hung up and Dad said, "Hornsby said it's moving slowly because they're looking into other cases of sexual deviance against children committed by diplomats while posted overseas."

"How many cases are there?" Mom sounded appalled.

"Hornsby said he knows of two in recent years. He didn't say much more. He doesn't have the power to make Washington move more quickly. So we have to keep working with that asshole." From the muffled sound of his voice, I knew he was holding his face with his hands, the way he did when he was stressed, the way I saw him do all the time, ever since that horrible night when I revealed the truth about Mr. Mulcahy. "Hornsby said for now we just have to deal with it and try to get back into the swing of things."

Back to work, back to school, back to the beach on Sundays. Back to the ambassador's pool, back to kids bickering over who was gonna be Marco, and who was gonna be Polo, back to adults shouting "No running!" as we chased each other around the slippery tile deck.

Everyone tried to move on.

But it was hard, because so many quotidian activities fell under the shadow of Mr. Mulcahy's crimes. Now, whenever we went swimming, parents sat on the side of the pool, their feet dangling in the water, passing sun tan oil back and forth, murmuring their theories. *Maybe Mr. Mulcahy was a eunuch! Or maybe Geraldine refused to have sex with him! Maybe she knew all along but didn't say anything to keep him off of her!*

They kept their eyes glued to the water, even though there was never an adult man in the pool with their children now that Bill Mulcahy was gone.

"I'll never trust a man again," one woman said.

"And certainly not with my children," said another. "Funny, though, my daughter seems to have already forgotten about it. But I don't know how I'll ever recover."

Devastated.

It probably *was* easier for the children to move on than the parents, because it was nothing new. The kids had been absorbing the abuse in a slow, drawn-out way over years. The chronic stress of being repeatedly molested was like the *drip drip drip* of chemo, poison infiltrating the body, killing one part of the person while toxifying the part that survived. Of course, chemo has a benefit: it kills cancer. Sexual abuse not only kills self-esteem and self-image, it adds a defense mechanism that forever alters the ability to trust, to be intimate, to love.

One day, an older child from the Embassy community cornered me in the changing room at the pool.

"Let me look at you," she said, scanning my body from head to toe. "A pervert wouldn't want *me*," she said. "What made him want *you?*"

"Cause she's *pretty*," another kid jumped in, "and men love pretty girls." Her tone was not mocking or defensive. She stated it as a matter of fact, something she herself had clearly overheard.

Prettiness begets molestation: what a message. But it was a message I internalized, one that would take years and years for me to let go of. I didn't have the distance or the language to understand that this was just more victim blaming, more "whatever you do, don't hold the abuser responsible."

This moment was so seminal that even now, writing this book, I can still hear their voices: the *tsk tsk* of the first one's tongue as she judged my flesh and the pragmatic tone of the other as she explained it was all somehow the fault of my body.

But I was ready. "Because I'm pretty," I said, "*and* because I'm so fucking brilliant."

They burst into laughter as I skipped off, my whole self on overdrive, pumped with the adrenaline of my rebuttal and my clever capacity to hide my shame. At only twelve years old, I was already the master of blasé coolness; it was the only analgesic to the humiliation of exposure.

Without warning, six months after Mr. Mulcahy was sent back to Washington, the conclusion of the investigation arrived by cable. Dad came home from work early one evening to tell us the news.

There was no federal law against pedophilia.

And if there was a law in the Ivory Coast, Mr. Mulcahy had diplomatic immunity.

He would not be prosecuted.

He wouldn't even lose his job.

The case was closed.

The community plunged back into crisis. As if it wasn't horrific enough to discover that a beloved "friend" had been sexually abusing their children, it was even more unimaginable that the State Department was just going to let him get away with it.

The message was clear:

Protecting Mr. Mulcahy *was* important.

The sexual abuse of children was *not* important.

Acting with decorum as US diplomats *was* important.

Restitution for traumatized families was *not* important.

Two stories, both predicated on the abuse of power, running in perfect parallel. Mulcahy abused the children, and the State Department sealed the deal. Only when I became a parent myself would I understand how awful it was that the "adult" body these Embassy families depended on refused to help them in any meaningful way. Only as an adult would I understand that the State Department that controlled their entire lives was silencing them.

Getting ready for school one morning, I slammed my thumb in the door, bringing tears. Dad came down the hall at that moment, and when he saw me crying, assumed that it was about Mulcahy. Dad was not a touchy-feely type, and when he put down his briefcase to take me in his arms, saying, "It's going to be all right," I split in half, almost recoiling from this intimacy I wasn't accustomed to, while memorizing the feeling of being hugged this way, my face pressed against the satiny fabric of his necktie.

I yearned for Rose, yearned to tell my best friend about this new version of my parents. They were shell shocked, disoriented, and overwhelmed, dealing with a crisis of this magnitude in a foreign land. Even so, they tried to fight back. Telegrams went back and forth between Abidjan and Washington; phone calls were made from within the secret chambers of the United States Embassy to the State Department.

How can this be possible? And what about all the children he will come in contact with going forward? What about recourse? What about accountability?

My parents insisted on this question for many weeks; I suppose other parents in the community did, too. But no one in Washington was concerned about that, and certainly not about the twelve-year-old girl that lived with him.

No one thought about Rose.

The cables that arrived in response to every one of my parents' demands for justice said the same thing:

CASE CLOSED.

In the same way no kid had been able to stand up to Mr. Mulcahy, not a single adult could stand up to the US State Department. As a gesture of "goodwill," though, the State Department transferred Mr. Mulcahy off the Africa desk, significantly reducing the chances of the victims' parents having to work with him.

And that was that.

Now you need to put the incident behind you, said the decision-makers in Washington. *You need to carry on with a good attitude. Keeping a positive image is part of representing your country abroad.*

Over time, the number of people who lived in Abidjan when the Mulcahys did got diluted, and at the community level, the story faded into the background. In my family, the story faded, too, but only from the surface. The wounds were there, bloody and oozing, but we willed them to invisibility because no one had the psychological capacity to deal with it anymore.

It was easier to just be together but suffer alone.

Well, my parents seemed to be suffering, as did my sisters, who inevitably also absorbed their pain. The Mulcahy drama had been cataclysmic in so many ways, depending on whether you were the parent, the sibling, or the victim. But the trauma that befell the other members of the family is not my story to recount, and were I to even try, I'd undoubtedly miss the mark. Trauma is so deeply personal that I prefer to keep my focus on the only story I know by heart—and that is the events as I lived them.

And what I remember vividly from that time, as we all moved on, was feeling relieved and—dare I admit it?—*happy.*

Finally, we could stop talking about it. I had much more important things to focus on. I had turned thirteen, and though I still didn't have my period, I was a hotshot. I had gotten my ears pierced, some disco pants, a sassy attitude, and a new group of best friends. Together, we did all the stuff my parents forbade me to do, and more. I hung out with those "sleazebags" at the Hotel Ivoire, made out with them at the pool, the movies, and under the stairway that led to the bowling alley. I rode on the backs of their motorcycles. I tried puffs of their cigarettes. My parents couldn't stop me, no way.

Well, they tried, by acting all strict and saying no to so many parties, outings, any get together if they thought there would be boys present. But their strategy only propelled me to tell lies—extravagant, complicated lies, because there was no way I was going to miss out on all the fun. The world was teeming with cute guys, and their attention was magnetic. It filled me with a sense of power I was only just discovering, watering the seed of that destructive idea that if I wasn't appealing to men, I wasn't anything.

Men love pretty girls.

If a guy showed interest in me, I was winning. But if he lost interest, I was losing. As I was if pimples erupted on my face or if I had a bad hair day or if any other human imperfection manifested. I had to be sexy. And if I couldn't have full control over my body, I could tighten my game with my attitude, and so I learned to flirt, suggest, and entice.

Years later, I would understand how my abuse at the hands of Mr. Mulcahy led me to confuse sexual attention with love, and because I believed that sex was the only reason anyone would ever actually love me, my willingness to be sexual, even when I didn't want to, was driven by desperation. I could not remember ever feeling like I was deserving of love just because I was a human being, existing on this planet. I saw love as something I had to earn by being beautiful, desirable, and willing to not just give my body over but to use it to affirm men. I wasn't just a sparkling object for them to play with, but an object that responded, always in the affirmative. You did not need to be a good lover to me; you could be as inconsiderate and repulsive as you liked and I would still play along and lead you to believe that it was just wonderful to be with you. But even girls who haven't been abused get caught up, to varying degrees, in that same confusion. That's what we learn, from magazines, movies, social media, and people around us who keep the attention focused on our appearance and how we measure up in the eyes of men.

To the naked eye, I was just another teenager, struttin' her stuff. But the boy-craziness, the precocity, were the only things I had to mitigate the pain of everything that had happened: the public humiliation, my parents' despair, the abandonment of the State Department, losing my best friend.

Especially losing Rose.

I still thought about her sometimes, but as a memory from my childhood, which had ended a long time ago.

CHAPTER THIRTEEN

Geneva, Switzerland 2017

I hurried toward the lake, the swish of traffic in the background barely perceptible over the noise in my head following the session with Dr. Invicta. For so many years I had struggled to understand that paradox inside me: feeling shy and inadequate, yet acting bold, flaunting my body, fiending for the approval of men. I had studied Winnicott in grad school, and yet I hadn't ever really dissected *my* true and false selves. I had always thought I was so self-aware, but the current circumstances were forcing me to face my crumbling defenses.

At the lake, I walked the path that bordered the water. The waves were high and choppy today. A family of swans bobbed like bath toys, along with so many memories that bobbed in and out of my mind.

Men love pretty girls.

I had gone to West Africa as a ten-year-old whose main preoccupation was becoming the next Judy Blume. By the time I hit adolescence, I was outside of my own skin, constantly evaluating whether I measured up sexually, playing a role I didn't fully understand, one that involved mirroring whatever desire the boy in front of me expressed.

I was terrified of not measuring up, of not being as sexy or sweet as the compliments that spilled from their lips. It was sexiness, and that sweet accommodation that I slid into so automatically, that inspired their love. The major missing piece to this logic was the knowledge that securing their love did not have to be my objective. That was the problem: being an object of desire had become the only objective that I truly believed in anymore.

The more I realized the extent of my developmental wound, the more painful memories bubbled up. I still marveled at how, despite my professional training, I could have remained so walled off from my own trauma, but I had stopped beating myself up about it. What mattered was that the walls were coming down, exposing all of those experiences and feelings that I had kept so tightly compartmentalized for so long.

My thoughts jumped to my twenty-fifth birthday, exactly one year before meeting Tano. It was a hot August day in Seattle, and I had gone for a swim at Green Lake. While toweling off, deep in thought about the essay I would write for my graduate school application, a man approached me. He must have been in his late forties—how old that seemed at the time!—and he had a big smile on his face.

"I've gotta tell ya," he said. "You are drop dead gorgeous …"

I smiled, flattered.

"… Except for those fat thighs. You should do something about it."

Even now, I could cry, remembering the hurt cleaving me in two. Though one part of me knew it was completely fucked up that this random man (who incidentally didn't have such a great physique himself) felt entitled to dissect me this way, another part of me wanted to cut my thighs off right there on the beach.

Men love pretty girls.

The lump in my throat turned into tears; they clouded my vision but did not spill down my cheeks. I wiped them away and stared out across the lake, as rough and choppy today as the many oceans I had crossed in my lifetime. It was suddenly so clear to me: It wasn't just moving around the world that had honed my capacity for reinvention. It was my relationship with Mr. Mulcahy that had taught me to show up as someone I thought I needed to be, rather than who I really was.

My thoughts were abruptly interrupted by the sound of screams, fast approaching, high pitched and relentless. It was a woman pushing a stroller with two small children strapped into it. They seemed to be identical twins. Even their howls were perfectly matched, along with the crimson of their faces and the rhythm of their thrashing. I smiled to convey my sympathy, but she averted her gaze: the shame of the mother whose children disrupt the peace. A few feet later she released them from their torture, and their rage turned to joy. I watched as they waddled down the path, their glee pure, unfettered. The mother turned back and said with palpable pride, "That's how they usually are. I don't know what got into them this morning."

The true and the false selves. That's how it started: take a free-spirited child and strap them down. Now my thoughts segued to Tano and a long-ago night in New Orleans. I had called him from the payphone at the back of Fat Harry's Bar, midshift, to tell him I was having a panic attack. One of the tables I was serving was toasting their buddy who had died of AIDS, and my hypochondria had gone into overdrive.

I got off shift early, and Tano came to meet me. The car was parked up Saint Charles Avenue, and we got into the back seat so that he could hold me while I sobbed.

"Something is wrong with me!"

He caressed my face. "*Loca.* There's nothing wrong with you!"

"There is, I just know it," I cried, barely able to catch my breath. "I'm sure I'm dying."

He pulled me to his chest. "If you are dying, I will stay by your side until the end."

It was the kindest, most compassionate thing anyone had ever said to me, and I clung to him like Saran wrap as a street car rattled by, shaking the leaves from the oaks onto our windshield.

I started walking slowly towards home, thinking about that night in New Orleans. That was my true self who had shown Tano all of my fear and the depths of my fragility. I hadn't ever been that real with a man before, and for a time, our relationship was deeply healing. But his rejection of my origins had sent that true part into hiding. Sometimes she ventured out to try and reconnect with him, but there were so many geopolitical dramas, and the good feeling between us was constantly under threat. Was I just thin skinned? He thought so, thought it was ridiculous I would take his political views personally. But that wasn't the issue, especially because I agreed with him most of the time. What injured me was his expectation that I wouldn't be affected by all the limitations his political views imposed on our togetherness. That because I was American I should just suck it up and deal with the scorn and criticism, the never-ending stream of denigrating things said about the place I came from. That I didn't deserve empathy when terrible things like 9/11 happened. It seemed the essence of prejudice.

Now that I had broken free, I could see clearly how I had relinquished all of my boundaries to stay in his good stead and keep our relationship together. I wasn't so naïve that I didn't know, as it played out, that something unhealthy was in process. But that was the nature of the beast I had been locked in struggle with since I was ten years old: the very things that stripped my sense of self-worth attached me even tighter to whoever was peeling it off, one criticism at a time.

Rain clouds moved in over the lake, and I hurried back to my apartment, a sense of clarity and purpose rising. I still had time before my first appointment, and I wanted to do some writing about this. At home I turned on my computer and while I waited for it to boot up, prepared a sandwich and a cup of tea. I took them to my office and had just started to type when I heard it.

"*Uuuuuuuuuuuh… Uuuuuuuuuuuh.*"

Oh my God, was someone hurt? I sprang to my feet and flung open the door to the stairwell of the building. The air was cool and quiet. I stood still, listening.

"Uuuuuuuuuh … Uuuuuuuuuh … UUUUUUUUH, oh God, yes."

What the hell?

I closed the door and moved toward the noises. I wasn't sure if they were coming from Agatha or Ursula's room until the bed springs started squeaking.

Oh. The realization of what was happening kicked into place. Those were not sounds of pain.

It was Agatha. *Geez.* I hadn't stated it explicitly, but when I established my rule about being careful about bringing guests into the house because of my twelve-year-old son, I assumed they understood it wasn't their elderly aunt I was concerned with.

Fortunately, Lorenzo was at school, so I went back to my office and waited. Half an hour later, I heard murmuring at the front door and then the click of the latch. I waited a minute and then went to find Agatha. She was in the kitchen, wearing nothing but an oversized sweatshirt that fell to mid-thigh. Her legs were stout but shapely, and a thin gold chain encircled her left ankle. Her hair was tousled and wild, and combined with the sight of her bare legs and feet, she oozed sex. I wondered if she was naked underneath that sweatshirt.

"Agatha? This is awkward … but, um …"

She was pulling food from the fridge, and she laughed as she turned toward me, pushing her hair from her face. "The guy?"

"Uh, yeah. I mean, I'm glad you were having such a great time—"

"Totally faking," she said, popping a grape in her mouth. "Sorry for the noise. It was going on and on, and I was just trying to hurry him up."

I had to laugh. "Who was it?"

"Someone I met on Tinder. He wanted a second date, but I said no." I must have had a strange look on my face, because she added, "I know it's harsh, but I'm not going to pity-date someone. I'm picky."

But I wasn't thinking she was harsh. I was thinking about how I had never been harsh enough. Picky was not even in my vocabulary when I was in my twenties, rolling indiscriminately from one relationship to the next, with little selection criteria beyond their interest in me, constantly adapting so that I wouldn't lose an opportunity for connection. Agatha's confidence was impressive, though it struck me that while she was confident enough to do that, she hadn't been honest when the sex wasn't fulfilling.

"Are you on Tinder?" Agatha asked. "Or any of the dating apps?"

"Me?" I felt my face turn pink. "Oh no, I … I haven't been thinking about dating."

"Give it a go!" Agatha said. "It's fun!"

"I wouldn't know where to begin," I said, my mind already playing Whac-A-Mole with all the insecurities the mere suggestion of dating produced at this point. Namely, wrinkles, sags, and the fact that the last time I had tried to attract a man, I was twenty years younger. Sometimes I thought about Dennis, the trucker in Arizona, but that seemed like a fluke, or just some spontaneous, heatstroke-induced delusion.

Agatha whipped out her phone and pulled up Tinder. "Look!" she said, doing some fancy thumb work on the screen. "I'll change my settings to men your age so you can see—"

I held up my hand. "It's OK. I know what Tinder is like. I have a friend with an account." My mind flashed to Olivia and the hours she spent scrolling.

"I hope you try it!" Agatha winked and headed back to her room, the bowl of grapes in her hand, as though Dionysus himself were waiting for her.

I had three sessions back-to-back, and then Lorenzo came home from school. We chatted about his day for a few minutes while he slathered Nutella on bread, folding the pieces and shoving them in his mouth so fast I said, "Slow down! Are you looking for a way to choke?"

He laughed through his mouthful, wiped his chocolatey hands on the dishtowel, and went in search of his skateboard. I had two more sessions before I was done for the day. When my last client left, I rummaged through the cupboards and fridge, looking for dinner ideas but barely seeing the food. I was still thinking about dating. And I hadn't been totally straight with Agatha, because I had been thinking about it for a while. It was hard not to, overhearing her and Ursula giggling about their hook-ups. And Olivia had been trying for months to get me on Tinder by regaling me with stories of her jam-packed dating life. Since that long-ago morning when she whispered into the phone, she'd had multiple brief liaisons with men that each seemed to have a shelf life of a month before they went bad.

I kept telling her I was far too busy to even consider it. And she knew my days were long, that I didn't turn down any requests for appointments, committed as I was to being financially stable. Between work and the kids, when was I supposed to date?

That said, I had been thinking about men. Like, how convenient it would be to have one around to attend to certain tasks that Tano had always done for me: changing the lightbulbs in high ceiling lamps, fixing the toilet that refused to flush, programming the television. It wasn't just financial management that was forcing me to grow up, and fast. It seemed every week there was a new household conundrum to deal with, and I thanked God for YouTube and its thousands of instructional videos that had been my guide as I started navigating these questions on my own. Before Tano and I separated, I didn't realize it was going to be so much work, being him. Now, it was *me* screwing the door handle back on, oiling the squeaky hinge, ordering the replacement part for the dishwasher, unclogging the sink, taking out the recycling. It was *me* paying bills, filing insurance claims, studying the bank account to make sure there was enough money set aside for the taxes coming up soon.

I put a frozen quiche in the oven. Then I went back to my office and put my feet up on the desk. I called Lorenzo at the skate park to tell him to come home now; dinner would be ready in half an hour. Then I called Olivia. She answered on the first ring and said, "I'm so upset. Alan is ghosting me."

Alan was her latest Tinder conquest. Just a week earlier, she reported that he'd said he was falling in love with her.

"Are you sure?"

"Well, he hasn't answered my messages for two days. I started thinking something had happened to him. But his secretary said he was in a meeting." She sighed. "Asshole."

"What are you going to do?"

"Stalk his social media and … oh hell, what can I do? Cry myself to sleep? I didn't even like him that much. I just wasn't expecting to be dumped without a word. So, when are you going to get online?"

I snorted. "Your story isn't exactly inspirational."

"It's a numbers game. And I'm an optimist. I've got a date set up for tomorrow night. But enough about me. How are you?"

I told her about Agatha's little performance that afternoon, and she laughed. "I mean, c'mon, haven't you—"

"Of course. Who hasn't?"

Olivia launched into a story about the last time she had faked. It sounded like that scene from *When Harry Met Sally*. But my mind drifted to other things I'd overheard Agatha and Ursula discuss recently, conversations about their salaries, vying for raises, being pissed off that they weren't being paid enough. When I was twenty-six, I wasn't vying for any raise. I was vying to secure a man.

Olivia got to the end of her anecdote, and I laughed on cue, but it came out more like a sob. "Oh, honey," she said. "What is it?"

"I don't know," I sniffled. "Something about that interaction with Agatha triggered me. Something about her confidence. It's just growing pains. I guess I'm comparing myself to her. To both of them."

"To the *renters*? What's to compare?"

"They're just so in charge of themselves. When I was twenty-six, I was pathetic. It's embarrassing!"

"But that was so long ago! Look how far you've come!"

"It's retroactive embarrassment," I said, remembering my first year of marriage. I told Olivia how Tano and I had arrived in Nairobi, and I had flailed around, completely miserable because I couldn't find work. This put me at great odds with Tano, who did nothing *but* work. I cringed thinking about how much time I had spent, when he was elbows deep in epidemics—famine, cholera, hemorrhagic fever—trying to seduce him, to win back the desire he had shown me the first months we were together. It had felt urgent; without the sex, our relationship had become thin, disconnected, and I could vividly recall the desperation I'd felt for his attention.

"Anyway," I added, "It's silly to obsess about the past. It's just that with these two girls in the house, I can't help but wonder sometimes how Nairobi would have gone—how our whole marriage would have gone—if Tano and I had started out on equal ground."

"You mean if you'd both had jobs?"

"No, if we'd both had confidence."

Olivia sighed. "The million-dollar question."

After we hung up, I lay on the sofa and watched a spider cross the ceiling, thinking about the conversation with Olivia. It wasn't regret I felt, it was more like post-factum self-awareness. And good things *had* emerged from that first terrible year of marriage. My depression and loneliness had driven me into a writing group, and I'd actually managed to write a novel. A shitty, ridiculous novel that never saw the light of day, but still. God, it was visceral, the memory of typing THE END and feeling such exhilaration … until I read it through for the first time. It was so bad. How had that happened? Clearly, I had fooled the writing group by sharing choice dramatic passages. Or maybe they had just lied when they told me how they loved it; come to think of it, anyone listening in on our meetings would have thought we were all Pulitzer Prize winners, the way we raved about each other's work. Alone with my manuscript, though, I had seen the lie. My book was hardly a page turner; it even bored *me* to tears.

The front door slammed, breaking my reverie.

"Mom?"

"I'll be right there, sweetheart!"

"*Mom!* There's a fire!"

I threw open the door, expecting to see flames. But all that greeted me was the smell of burning quiche. I raced to the kitchen and opened the window. I was still contemplating a plan B for dinner when a bat flew in. The last time this happened, Tano had dealt with it, cool as a cucumber, done and dusted in five minutes. I spent the next hour shrieking and cursing, trying to flap it out with an umbrella. Finally I managed and then went straight to the shower, horror fantasies of rabies mixing in my mind with the notion of maybe getting on Tinder after all. But it made me nervous. Dating seemed like the writer's workshop: for other people, not for me. What if no one wanted me? Deep down, I feared no one would ever love me again.

The thought itself invoked pain, followed by an elaborate sexual fantasy with a faceless stranger. But what the hell was I thinking? In my younger years, that tactic had rarely produced anything other than compulsivity. If I got on Tinder, there would be so many chances to spiral into old patterns. I had always been the type to declare moderation and then smoke all the cigarettes, eat all the cookies, drink the whole bottle of wine. Hell, I had gone to New Orleans determined to take a break from dating and ended up married instead.

This is dangerous, I told myself. *Don't do it.*

An hour later, I signed up.

CHAPTER FOURTEEN

Cairo, Egypt 1983

Just when it seemed things had gone back to normal in Abidjan, Dad got his new assignment: we were moving to Egypt. Mom tried to make it sound like it was going to be so wonderful to start fresh, but I was bereft. The Mulcahy drama had exploded eighteen months earlier, and I couldn't bear more upheaval.

Even so, a few months later, it was impossible to not feel excited by the sight of the pyramids and the Sphinx, visible from the air, as we circled over Cairo. But the thrill was quelled once we settled in and discovered that compared to Abidjan, Cairo was a difficult place to live. The city was sprawling, dusty, and terrible traffic made the distances so much worse. The Embassy assigned us an apartment in a neighborhood called Ma'adi, so close to our new school we could see it from the window. This was convenient for the three of us to walk to school, and for Mom, who had been hired as the school librarian. The US Embassy was downtown in Garden City, so Dad had a veritable commute, back and forth every day, in the Embassy shuttle. That relaxed, easy feel of life in Abidjan, with the living room doors thrown open to the garden, no longer existed for there were strict timetables and a different expectation of how to be in a conservative Muslim culture.

And that was not the only radical change. After four years in the warm, cosy atmosphere of the International School of Abidjan, being tossed into Cairo American College—a big American high school with all the predictable cliques—was like being thrown to the lions. I had breezed into CAC wearing the clothes and the attitude that made me cool in Abidjan, only to find that it would not fly in this new environment.

"Slut," a horrible girl named Britney hissed whenever we crossed paths in the hallway. The movie *Mean Girls* was still more than twenty years from existence, but Britney epitomized the trope, picture perfect with her makeup and fancy outfits and ugly, cruel character. She enlisted all of her friends to target me: "slut" was their favorite slur, with "dumb blonde" as second runner up, and "ditz" and "airhead" tied for third place.

I steeled my gaze and acted like I didn't care, but inside I ached as the harassment eroded my self-image. But I didn't know who, if anyone, I could talk to at school about the bullying, and there was no way I would confide in my parents that I was being treated as the school slut. Even though it was unfounded, I felt guilty and ashamed, and some combination of stress, adolescence, and the carryover of the Mulcahy trauma made me want to hide it from them.

"Slut, slut, slut," Britney hissed, as we crossed each other one day at the school gate. She was on her way in, carrying a big bag of pom-poms, undoubtedly something for her stupid cheerleading routine. I was on my way out, having gone to the library to ask my mother's permission to go home for the afternoon. I told her I had cramps, though I really just needed a break.

Mom had given me cash to pick up some groceries for dinner at the mini mart on the ground level of our apartment building, and I went through the aisles quickly, tossing things into the basket, barely aware of my actions. Next to the checkout was the bread, a basket big enough to sit in, heaped with fluffy, white loaves. I grabbed the biggest one I could see and handed it to the cashier.

At home, alone, I dropped the groceries on the kitchen counter, changed into my pajamas, and put on the *Guilty* album. I skipped straight to "Woman in Love," lay down on the sofa, and sobbed. I missed Abidjan, where I knew who I was and where I had real friends. When the song ended, I floated to the kitchen. Standing at the counter, I slathered hunks of bread with peanut butter and jelly, shoveling them into my mouth so fast jelly dripped down my chin and onto my pajama top. I couldn't slow down. It tasted so good, the squish of soft dough between my teeth so satisfying, I just wanted more, just wanted to feel good for a few minutes. I devoured the entire loaf before the *Guilty* album had even finished playing. I was stuffed, but I felt better.

That night, Mom asked, "Where's the bread?"

"Oh, sorry, I forgot to buy it," I said, my hand resting on my stomach, still packed solid with dough.

Binging became a daily event. Soon enough, my skinny frame filled out, and my clothes got tight. A tenth grader I had a crush on told me I'd be pretty if I just lost ten pounds. He said it with bravado, as though he was paying me a compliment of the highest order, and I fell straight into line.

"Thank you!" I said in a sweet voice, all smiles and gratitude, even as inside, I was crumpling. My weight was a blemish on my beauty was a blemish on my value was a blemish on my very right to exist.

How terrible to be trapped in this body! I hated it, really hated it, and I'd stand in front of the mirror in my underwear, grabbing the flesh on my belly, grabbing my thighs from behind to create the illusion of the thinness I aspired to. *Seventeen* provided all the workout plans I needed, but it was so hard to get motivated.

I started smoking; I'd heard it was a great way to get off food. For a few days, I tried that instead of peanut butter and jelly, but soon I was back to eating the whole, slathered loaf, dessert to the cigarettes I sucked down as the main course.

Then my friend Liz, a transplant from Maine who was also new that year, bought diet pills at a pharmacy. She divided the pack between us. Wow, they really worked! Never mind I could no longer sleep at all and when I got out of bed in the morning, after an entirely sleepless night, I was still buzzing. But I was not eating, and that was the most important thing. Then Liz's mom found the pills and freaked out; apparently, we were on amphetamines. She flushed them down the toilet, and my desperation mounted.

How would I lose weight?

It seemed impossible until *Seventeen* delivered the answer: bulimia!

A full article on this tragic disorder afflicting thousands of teenage girls in America every year was a perfect instruction manual. It outlined exactly how to do it as it earnestly explained why you must never.

Goodbye despondency about my fat, disgusting body. Now I could binge away on my beloved PB&J, *and* bags of barbecue flavored Chipsys, and Twix, Snickers, and Mars bars. I bought this contraband at the kiosk up the road, owned by the middle-aged man who grabbed my hand when he gave me my change, stroking my palm with his thumb.

"*Helw awi*," he breathed. *Very beautiful.*

I knew he would do this, and I didn't care. It was gross—all the girls agreed, because he did it to all of us—but privately, it made me feel better about myself, reassured me that I might be loved one day. My big sister and I shared a group of friends, and we gallivanted around Cairo to a chorus of *helw awi*s, and other gestures, cars driving slowly by, men leering at us, licking their lips like hungry wolves. Every now and again, a window would come down, showcasing a waggling dick.

When that happened, we clutched each other and ran—*Ewwwww!*—scream-laughing at the sight of a penis. *Hilarious!* It didn't dawn on any of us we could be in actual danger. We made a huge joke of it instead, using a tape recorder to dub over my cassette of James Taylor singing "You Got A Friend" to you've got a … THROBBING PENIS!

We shrieked with laughter at our little modification. We laughed so hard we gasped for breath, doubled over, clutching our sides, high-fiving each other for our cleverness. At fourteen, it didn't occur to me that Mr. Mulcahy and the men chasing us down the road were all part of a brotherhood of abusers, that every single one of these behaviors could be plotted on a continuum from bad to worse. The Politics of Patriarchy class I would take at Mount Holyoke just a few years later would give me the language for so many things I previously hadn't questioned. But it would be years before I could see how all these dots connected and how insidiously the constant objectification was shaping my self-image.

By the end of the first year in Cairo, I loved it. It was home now. I never wanted to leave, even though I still hated my school and the wicked Britney who ran it. The life I loved was outside the school gates. With my big sister and our friends, we took horseback riding lessons at the Pyramids, did the Jane Fonda workout tape, and spent weekends drunk at parties and nightclubs filled with boys boys boys!

Pub 13, Bel-air, Jacky's at the Hilton Hotel in downtown Cairo. We showed up at these venues, blasted out of our minds, to consort with guys who were much older: nineteen, twenty, even twenty-five! They moved in on us the way dust storms moved in on Cairo: with little warning and all at once. No one controlled any of this—not the establishments I frequented, not my parents, whom I lied to anyway—and I spun completely out of control.

Sophomore year, something amazing happened: I got nominated for the homecoming court! If I won, I'd be crowned princess of the tenth grade! Not that I wanted to be princess of the tenth grade, or of anything, really, at CAC. I had written off all those rah-rah events since day one of my stressful life at this school where I felt painfully separate, unable to fit in. But being nominated for this contest seemed like an olive branch—maybe I *could* be part of the crowd?

The proof came a few days after the nomination, when Shlomi, who was part of the National Honor Society, asked me to be his date!

He was two years older than me, smelled like garlic, and had terrible dandruff. Not once, ever, had I imagined going on a date with him. But he was one of those kids who had been at the school since kindergarten, which gave him an acceptance pass with all the cliques. Everyone liked him, even me, though the first time I ever actually spoke to him was when he invited me to the dance. But I already knew he wasn't one of *those* kids who went around acting like they owned the school, and the more I thought about it, why not? I could like him, if I just applied myself a little.

My parents said I could order a dress from the Penney's catalogue, and I chose it carefully, visions of myself as the perfect *Seventeen* girl in my mind. It was black taffeta, more glamorous than anything I'd ever owned; it would be the gown of my transformation.

But when it arrived and I lifted it from the box, my heart sank. The dress was stiff to the touch and shiny, and the fabric smelled like tar.

"Put it on," Mom said. "It probably just needs a little air and movement to fall right."

But zipped into it, I didn't become *Seventeen*-girl thin, with long bouncy hair, and no pimples. I looked like ten-pounds-too-heavy-to-be-pretty me, in a starchy, smelly dress.

I hung it in my closet, doubled down on the smoking, and tried to starve myself. I was desperate to be thinner, but the more I restricted, the more I binged, and soon I was throwing up multiple times per day. Excitement turned to dread.

The day of the dance, an enormous floral arrangement arrived at my door, with a card tucked between the leaves:

Looking forward to a pleasant evening. Shlomi.

It was such an adult gesture; it reminded me of the flower arrangements

Mom would receive in Abidjan after hosting lavish diplomatic receptions. It set the tone for how I thought I was supposed to be that evening, all grown up and serious, in my disappointing dress that, at least, no longer smelled.

Shlomi came to get me, looking dapper in a pin-striped suit, his hair curly with wet effect gel. All day I had talked myself into being excited about him, and I beamed at him when Dad snapped our photo. I *wanted* to be smitten. But as he pinned a rose on my dress and the fumes of his hair gel and cologne made me dizzy, I couldn't lie to myself: I wasn't attracted to him. Nor could I think of anything to say, and my face blazed in the dark of the backseat of his car, where he sat next to me, bantering in Arabic with his driver, for the sixty seconds it took to drive us from my apartment to the school.

The party was just getting started as we arrived, and after awkwardly dancing to "Girls Just Wanna Have Fun," a giddy expression plastered on my face, I escaped with my friends to the shadows outside the school gate, where we slugged back Omar Khayyam, the local wine bought on the cheap. They had cleverly disguised it in soda bottles that we passed around and then hid in the bushes, to be retrieved when we needed another shot of confidence. By the time we walked back into the dance, Shlomi was wet with sweat from dancing, and I was just drunk enough to actually enjoy stumbling around with him to the sounds of David Bowie and Prince booming through the gymnasium.

When the kid who was playing MC announced *I* had been chosen as tenth-grade homecoming princess, I was shocked. This was not the outcome I was expecting, and I was grateful to steady myself on Shlomi's arm as he walked me to the stage to be crowned.

En route, I caught Britney's eye, and she glared. *Slut.* Suddenly, I felt powerful. I may have been the dumb blonde slut, but I was the one standing up here, and I knew what it meant: guys wanted *me*. Take that, Britney! *Bitch!*

She averted her gaze when I glared back at her, and I took my final steps to the stage, actually feeling proud. I had passed the judgement of the masses!

The homecoming theme song was Bryan Adams's "Heaven," and like all the other princesses, I had to dance with my counterpart. The tenth-grade prince was a Bulgarian guy named Franck, and I put my head on his shoulder, though it was awkward because I was taller than he.

The song ended, and then the members of the homecoming court had to dance with their dates. Shlomi put his arms around my waist, and because he was taller than me, I could put my head on his shoulder without feeling like such a dork. Foreigner's "I Want to Know What Love Is" blasted through the room. My heart was longing for the feeling the song promised. I wanted to know what love was. I needed to convince myself about Shlomi. I was certain I could make it work if I could just get over feeling bored and not attracted.

The song ended and without missing a beat, Kool and the Gang ignited the auditorium with "Celebration." Shlomi broke into a moonwalk while students poured onto the floor from the sidelines. "Let's dance!" he said, shimmying around me. I loved the music and had danced in front of the mirror so many times at home. But now that I'd decided I wanted to be his girlfriend, I felt self-conscious. I was afraid I'd look stupid, clumsy, off beat, and so I said I was going for a cigarette, back in a minute.

I minced my way to the outskirts of the dance floor, looking for my friends. What I really needed was more of that wine. Then Dirk, the Dutch guy on the student council homecoming committee, came up to me.

"Congratulations! You happy?" He pulled my arm up in a victory pump and leaned in close to my ear. "You can thank me for the honor. Barely anyone voted for you."

I stepped back to see his face more clearly.

"You just aren't popular enough, but *I* think you're the most beautiful girl in the tenth grade. So, I rigged it."

What was he saying?

He leaned in again, tone lowered, as if anyone could hear him over the music. "A couple of us voted for you, like, a hundred times." He gloated, smug and self-congratulatory.

The auditorium was electrified; everyone was dancing and jumping and screaming along to the music. But I had frozen, my face in a terrible grin that I'd hold for so long my jaw would ache by the time I got home.

"Thank you *so* much," I said.

"It's our secret, yeah?"

"Of course."

He squeezed my arm. "Save a slow for me, yeah?" And then he weaved off through the crowd.

Suddenly, my friends were surrounding me. "Congratulations! How does it feel?"

"Great, really great," I answered, though my throat had tightened up like a noose.

I got so drunk that night I had to leave the dance to throw up in the bushes. The barf splashed on my dress, so I didn't go back in; I just stumbled home without even saying goodbye to Shlomi. Then I fretted all night about whether he'd hate me, but the following morning, a massive potted plant was delivered to my door.

Thanks for a pleasant evening.

Being tenth-grade princess and having gone to homecoming with Shlomi were stamps of approval. Now kids that never used to even look at me said hi. Even mean old Britney backed off. But I was in a constant state of dread: what if someone leaked the secret of the fake homecoming princess? Every time I walked through the school gates, I plastered on a congenial mien as a precautionary armor if ever the truth about me was revealed.

This was how I ended up going out with Dirk, even though I could not stand him for pulling me into his ballot-rigging hoax. And *ick* to the way he darted his pointy tongue in and out of my mouth, like a serpent. All I could think about when he was kissing me were the blackheads all over his shiny nose. I imagined those plump little plugs, ripe and ready for harvest, slipping from his skin onto mine, the way peas slip from their pods.

Then a new girl arrived on the scene, and apparently he thought she was the most beautiful of them all, because he started ignoring me. I saw him following her around between classes, and it was a huge relief.

So why did I feel like crying?

Nothing had changed. I still hated him.

But it was as though I had fallen from grace; I'd gone from most beautiful to least lovable. No one knew how much I hurt, not even my closest friends. The anguish was internal, something else to hide at all costs. Exposing my pain would tarnish my smiley, agreeable demeanor, my suit of armor, my greatest shield.

CHAPTER FIFTEEN

Geneva, Switzerland 2017

Even though I had been following Olivia's life on Tinder for many months, it still surprised me how easy it was to meet men. There were hundreds of them online, categorizable into the most predictable Geneva clichés: banker, trader, United Nations, humanitarian, ski instructor, independently wealthy. It was the epitome of instant gratification, though only marginally better than a game of blindman's bluff. Unlike the old children's game, however, on Tinder, everyone hoped to be caught.

Swipe, swipe, swipe!

Olivia and I approached the search for men like house hunters looking for a deal: *"What do you think of this one?"* We scrolled through their photos, pointing out the visible qualities, while trying to determine what hidden structural damage might hide behind that fresh coat of paint. I also underwent some refurbishing, trading in the grey costume of marital indifference—shapeless sports bras and period-stained underwear—for lacy undergarments that squeezed and lifted in all the key places.

Then I burst onto Tinder the way a circus performer bursts from a cannon.

I was also the ringmaster, coordinating the show, and the juggler, managing *five! six! seven!* text conversations, all at once. I did the trapeze act, swinging from one date to the next. Then came the contortionist: date after date I bent myself into pretzels, trying to find the connection.

The first handful of dates I went on were anodyne: an hour of chit-chat, followed by a handshake and a few vague, noncommittal follow-up text messages, until the communication fizzled. I felt a mixture of anxiety— *was I doing this all wrong?*—followed by a sense of being off the hook. It was so much easier to just stay home and watch Netflix. But I periodically thought about Dennis, from the hotel pool in Arizona, and how it had felt to feel attractive to a man.

So I kept swiping until I met Victor, a handsome South American diplomat. He was in his early fifties, never married, no children. Our first date turned into a marathon evening; what was supposed to be a quick drink became three. He talked a lot about his career and how it had interfered with every relationship he'd ever had. The longing in his voice, and his sad eyes, as he described the wonderful women who had gotten away, unable to tolerate the frequent travel and the late nights, touched me. I found myself thinking that I would never let him down the way those other women had. I knew how to be independent in a marriage, knew how to spend large swaths of time on my own. I turned the conversation to myself, and he gripped my hands across the table, his eyes becoming misty. "I could tell that you were different," he said.

The thrill of being chosen spread through my veins like liquid gold, softening me, opening me to his kisses when he suddenly lunged across the table, his chair making a loud scraping noise over the sultry music playing in the background. It was a Tuesday night and most tables were empty, thank God, because the immodest scene that played out was not one that I would have been proud of were any of my clients around.

"Come back to my place?" Victor murmured, when he finally pulled back.

"I'm hungry," I said, and he laughed.

"I'll make you an omelette."

"Let's have something here." He nodded, beckoning for the waiter. I knew that he had interpreted my statement to mean that we would go to his apartment once we had eaten. I needed to clarify this, but he had already gone back to recounting his diplomatic dealings, and I was already lost in images of the future: holding hands at the movies, getting married on the beach in some warm destination, cooking a meal in the beautiful kitchen of the house we would own together. I felt ravenous for love as I dug into the little plates placed before us holding olives, cheese, and freshly scrubbed radishes. They tasted so good, the crunch in my mouth releasing the sweet-sharp flavor, and I realized at some moment I wasn't even listening to him. He didn't notice; he just kept talking while I smiled and chewed.

Then the waiter was bringing the check, and Victor was shoo'ing away my hand as I reached for my wallet. "I would never let you pay!" he gasped, tapping his code into the credit card machine while the waiter looked away.

Outside, Victor took my arm and led me in the opposite direction of my house.

"I have to go home," I said, looking at the time on my phone, as if the proof of this statement lay in the numbers on the screen. 10:53 p.m.

"No!" he protested. "It's early! Come back to mine, and I'll drive you home later."

"I can't," I said, into his mouth as he kissed me. We went back and forth, playfully at first, until I detected the argument in his voice.

"You American women," he said, and I froze, catapulted backwards into one of my early dates with Tano when he had informed me American women were prude, unlike women from any other country where he had been. Then, as now, I knew this was ridiculous. And still, now, as then, this comment made me feel bad, made me want to prove that I wasn't that boring, unappealing thing being insinuated.

"Next date," I said, kissing him in a way intended to convey promise. The restaurant was only twenty minutes by foot from my apartment, but it took almost an hour for him to walk me home because of all the kissing and groping we stopped to do along the way. We parted ways, and by the time I had guzzled several glasses of water, washed my face and brushed my teeth, he had already sent me a string of text messages.

My sweater smells like you. I won't take it off all night.

Wish you were lying next to me right now.

I never believed in love at first sight. Until tonight.

This "love bombing" might have sounded some alarms, but his exalting statements about my utter wonderfulness soaked into every nook and cranny of my psyche, leaving me with the common sense of an English muffin. I pushed his comment about American women out of my mind. I pushed his pushiness out of my mind. Like a python before a snake charmer, I was mesmerized by his attention. The part of me that yearned to feel chosen believed everything Victor said; I would not allow myself to listen to any inner voice, faint though it was, saying, *"Stop fooling yourself."*

The night of our second date, I took time getting ready. I hadn't had sex for a very long time, and I felt giddy and self-conscious. Lorenzo was at Tano's for the evening, so I had Olivia on speakerphone and laughed uproariously at her advice. "Don't think," she instructed. "Drink!" Either Ursula or Agatha had an opened bottle of chardonnay in the fridge, and I crept into the kitchen like a thief, poured some into a mug, and then scurried back to my room.

Olivia was right; the wine relaxed me, such that by the time I got to the restaurant where Victor was waiting, I felt ebullient. American woman? I'd show him. What we ate and what we talked about are a blur; the unforgettable moments were the ones where our eyes locked, our knees touched, and our fingertips danced together across the table, little sparks of electricity flying between us.

When we stood up to leave, I felt woozy, unsteady on my feet. Had we actually drunk two bottles of wine? The night air brought cool relief, but he had chosen a restaurant near his apartment, and suddenly we were at his front door. I would have benefitted from more walking, but I didn't want to give the impression I was avoiding being alone with him again. His apartment was tidy and sparse, but the modern furniture was studied and lent an air of money. Victor took my coat and began to fiddle with a remote control. All at once the lights changed color from white to blue to pink, and Latin jazz burst through the speakers.

"More wine?"

"Water," I said, going into the bathroom and locking the door behind me. I looked around as I peed, peering at the labels of his cologne, toothpaste, hair wax. Then I stood and flushed, stepping back from the mirror before I pulled up my pants, trying to see my body, wondering how it would look to him. I stepped closer to the mirror and peered into my eyes. Was this my re-birth? Was I about to find love all over again?

Victor was waiting for me on the couch, shirt untucked, shoes nowhere to be seen. A glass of water sat on the table, and I sipped at it, suddenly shy. "Come," he whispered, reaching out his hand and pulling me towards him. We kissed, deep and slow, and then faster, until I suddenly was aware that something had switched. Victor's breathing was punctuated with moans—*mmmmmmhhhhhhhhh*—that lifted me out of the moment and into hyperawareness of the scene, as though I was outside of it, looking down. I stifled a giggle. The sounds he was making reminded me of the ones we made as kids, pretending to be grown up. But peering at him through half closed lids, Victor was clearly not playacting. In fact, he seemed to be elsewhere, lost in his own experience, no longer even aware of me, at the same time I was the critical component to what he was doing: kneading my breasts with his hands, biting at my neck and face, grinding his pelvis into mine.

"Oh baby," he groaned, squeezing my buttocks in a manner he certainly intended to be sexy. "Your ass, baby ..." His voice trailed off, and he gave another few firm squeezes. Then he smacked it. "You want a little spank, baby?"

I most definitely did not want a little spank, but I played along as if I liked it, feeling absurd as my flesh jiggled with each slap. Abruptly, he leapt up from the sofa and extended his hand to me. I took it and he pulled me to my feet and led me to the bedroom. It was dark except for the street lights coming in through the window, and I could see a determined look on his face when he pushed me back on the bed and climbed on top of me. He plunged inside me before I was ready, but I pretended to like it, choosing the same route as Agatha, wailing in phony ecstasy, craning my neck backwards and watching him watch me, a lubricious look on his face "Do you like that, baby?" he gasped, sweat dripping down his face onto mine. It was all so … *unpleasant* … and I couldn't wait for it to end, even as I encouraged him to keep jackhammering away at me. A larger vision was behind my eyes: me, the object of his desire, being exactly what he wanted, making him love me.

Finally, it was over. I stroked his back, feeling his heart pounding through his chest, wondering what would happen next. The low rumble of his snores provided the answer: nothing. My insides felt cavernous. The awareness in that moment of how little I knew this man filled me with loneliness, for Tano, for childhood, for … something else not yet definable.

What was I doing here? I had thought I wanted this. Hadn't I? Now in addition to this vast emptiness, I felt confused. What had I wanted?

I must have drifted off because the next thing I saw was the empty space next to me in bed, and the numbers of Victor's digital clock blinking 7:04 a.m. I lay there for a moment, registering the smell of coffee, willing him to bring me a cup. When that didn't happen, I pulled on my clothes and went to find him.

He was shoveling cornflakes in his mouth and watching a video on his phone.

"Good morning, handsome." I made my voice playful.

He barely glanced at me. "Help yourself to whatever."

I poured some coffee and sat down next to him. "Whatcha watching?"

"Cartoons," he said, laughing out loud as the characters on the screen bonked each other on the head, and then, abruptly, put his phone on the table. "I have football this morning. Some friends are coming by to pick me up in twenty minutes."

"Do I have time to shower?"

He looked at his phone. "It's cutting it close. Do you mind just—"

"Of course, it's fine." I arranged a carefree look on my face as he poured himself another cup of coffee, but I felt dismissed, and my face burned with embarrassment as I collected my things. Still, I acted blasé when we parted with no mention of a next meeting. I walked slowly home, replays of the evening running through my mind, insecurity mounting. Had it meant anything to him? Did I mean anything to him?

I hated my neediness, but was unable to stop myself from writing to him.

Thank you so much for a wonderful evening.

Short and courteous. No harm in that, and it provided him an opening to make things right between us.

At home I crawled into bed, and didn't wake until the early afternoon. The first thing I did was look at my phone. I could see Victor was online, though he hadn't read my message. Carmen sent news from London, and Olivia sent an update about her latest dating fiasco, and I kept simultaneous chit-chats going with them while monitoring Victor's account. He was on and off his phone all day too, but did not read my message. Lorenzo came home earlier than expected, which was a welcome relief; the rejection I was experiencing felt tremendous.

Afternoon turned to evening, and evening to night time. Victor did not read my message and did not write to me. I told myself I wouldn't spend any more time on him, but early the next morning, before I had even had my coffee, I lost control.

Good morning! Just checking in. Is everything OK?

By the time I was showered and dressed, he had read the message and, true to form, not answered. I grabbed my phone.

Victor! Why are you ignoring me? Did I do something to upset you? Why don't you answer?

I threw the phone down on the bed, hating myself for groveling. I tried to push Victor out of my mind. But as soon as Lorenzo left for school, I went back to my phone. He had replied.

Just because you write me a message doesn't mean I have an obligation to answer!

I called Olivia. "What did I do wrong?"

"Nothing. He's just an asshole."

"Yes, but, maybe if I ask him—"

"Do not respond!"

"But what if I offended him—"

"How would you have offended him?"

"I don't know." Uncertainty flooded my system, my mind reviewing every moment of our time together.

"Just get back in the saddle," Olivia said. "It's all you can do."

I moped around for a couple of days, but then I took her advice. Within two weeks of the fiasco with Victor, I had started up with Nigel, a Dubliner whose wife had just left him. He was handsome in a soap opera star sort of way, with thick, wavy hair and full, kissable lips. He wanted to spend as much time as possible together when we weren't with our kids. Nigel had three, all under the age of fourteen, whom he fretted about obsessively. What were they eating? Were they brushing their teeth three times a day? Were they getting a minimum of one hour of exercise per day? Were they following the rules about screen time?

After our fifth conversation in which he recited the same concerns, I had to admit to myself that Nigel was boring. I tried to deepen the conversation one evening as we walked around the lake. "I know how it feels to worry about the kids. I do it too. But I was wondering if maybe your worries run deeper?"

He stopped and looked at me. "What do you mean?"

"Well, you know," I stuttered, unsure if I should continue, judging from the defensive look on his face. "Splitting up is hard. I know how depressed I've felt, on and off, since I left my marriage—"

"I'm not depressed. Why would you even suggest that?"

There were a variety of reasons I had brought it up: The obsessing. The fact that he said he couldn't concentrate at work. That he drank beer every night. That we had only gone to bed together a few times, and he had been wracked with performance anxiety and erectile dysfunction.

When I described the situation to Dr. Invicta one morning, she said, "You're working hard to prove you enjoy being with this man. Why are you pretending?"

"Well, remember, I am the fake homecoming princess!"

"Why do you make fun of that? It's not funny. That was *traumatic*."

"Oh, come on, it's not 'traumatic' putting up with Nigel."

"I didn't say it was. But look at how history is repeating itself. You don't really enjoy being with Nigel. But you don't tell him. Just like with Dirk in Cairo, and how many others?"

The turn in conversation brought a rush of old feelings to the surface. Dr. Invicta named my homecoming saga as more trauma, though that wasn't such a revelation. What I hadn't considered was my response to it. Why hadn't I reacted differently to Dirk, if not publicly, then privately? A different type of girl might have told him to go fuck himself, instead of acting grateful for his "help." I shuddered, remembering his fishy breath and how he slobbered all over me. With that came the memory of that terrible fear of exposure, still so vivid even after so many years.

I felt some mix of rage and despondency. How was it that at only fifteen years old, Dirk already felt entitled to get whatever he wanted, whereas I, at age fifteen, already felt powerless? How I yearned to go back in time and teach that fifteen-year-old girl to say, *"Take your ballot and shove it."*

Dr. Invicta was correct; I *was* doing the same thing with boring old Nigel. "You're right. Maybe I should dump him."

"All I'm saying is that you should stop wasting your time on men you don't want to be with. Get involved with yourself."

"I don't know how!" I wailed.

"Yes, you do. Because you're already doing it, in your devotion to the things you care about. Like being a mother. A therapist. A writer."

I considered what she said. "You're right. But I still feel trapped."

She leaned forward in her seat. "My dear, you are *not* trapped. All you have to do is tell him you don't want to go out with him anymore."

I just stared at her.

"Did you hear what I said?" she pressed. "Are you going to keep putting what Nigel wants before what you want?"

I knew what the answer should be, but I felt incapable of disappointing him. Because no matter how much Nigel exhausted me, I *wanted* him to like me. The idea that he might stop filled me with anxiety. I tried to explain this to Dr. Invicta.

"You're in a regressive confusion," she said. "The apprehension around disappointing Mr. Mulcahy was something far bigger than a ten-year-old could manage. You accommodated him to stay in good standing; that's what abused children learn to do. But you're a grown woman, and you *don't* have to accommodate Nigel. You can end it and part ways cordially. Nothing bad will happen."

She made it sound so simple. I left the session feeling anxious, knowing it couldn't go on like this with poor, depressed Nigel, but still incapable of telling him that. I used the application for the writer's workshop as an initiation to the larger discussion that would eventually have to take place.

I'm going to hole up on Saturday and Sunday to get some writing done, I wrote in a text message. *Did I tell you I'm applying to a writing conference? With Alistair Grand!*

OK.

I just really need to get these pages written. The conference isn't for several months, but we're supposed to submit pages from our manuscript with the application.

OK. Let me know when you're free.

I was assuming he'd ask me something about the workshop, but he turned the subject back to his failed marriage. *You'll never believe what my ex did now!*

I extricated myself from a long text exchange about his wife, annoyed by his lack of curiosity. A few hours later, he called.

"My wife called! She wants to get together to talk! There's still hope!"

"Oh!" I said, taken aback not only by this twist, but with the way he shared this news with such glee.

"I'll get back in touch if it doesn't work out."

When we got off the phone, I called Olivia. "What is with these guys?" she said. "*'I'll get back in touch if it doesn't work out?'* Does he think you'll be sitting there waiting for him?"

I scoffed along with her, though I couldn't help feeling rejected. A weekend went by in which, apart from work and taking care of Lorenzo, I managed little more than flipping through Netflix, thinking about all the women I knew who came to *me* for advice, believing I was so evolved. *Take my advice, I'm not using it!* I thought, pained by the discrepancy between what I knew and what I did when it came to my own self-care.

But it was time to stop feeling bad. I needed to get back to the manuscript and the application to Alistair Grand's workshop. *Get involved with yourself,* Dr. Invicta kept saying. I hadn't really thought of it in those terms, but when I got off of Tinder to free up time to write, I could see clearly how much time and energy all that dating used up. Off of Tinder, I suddenly had a lot more time to work on the manuscript, and the process of telling the story was giving me new insight on the way the abuse at the hands of Mr. Mulcahy had shaped my life. But the deeper I delved into that painful history, the more I realized I was writing a story that I had not yet transcended. All of those self-image problems that drove me to seek the attention of men, to place myself before them as a sexual object rather than a whole person who saw herself as the subject of her own life, were ongoing. And it was only a matter of time before that compulsion took over again.

Swipe, swipe, swipe!

First there was Pierre, then Tomasso, then Luke, and then Gary. Four completely different men, from different cultural and educational backgrounds, yet every relationship followed the same pattern: get blasted together, have a lot of sex, wait for the situation to implode. I knew I was behaving recklessly, but there was an automaticity to my behavior that made it impossible to slow down. I justified it by saying to Olivia, "I know I'm out of control, but at least it's the fun kind of out of control!"

We tee-hee'ed together over that one, but deep down, I felt the old anguish. The previous weekend I'd given my latest conquest a lap dance. "You're a dream come true," he whispered, and I felt intoxicated by my power over him. But when he wanted to go for a walk in the mountains the following day, I came up with an excuse. I couldn't imagine spending time with him sober and fully clothed. I was afraid he wouldn't like me that way; deep down, I didn't believe there could be any interest in me beyond my naked body and the way it could be used for his pleasure.

Dr. Invicta said I was hiding behind all the sex and partying; that I was terrified of intimacy. "You are so preoccupied with whether these men want you, you are missing the real question: do you want them?"

She was incredibly skillful at putting words to things I had always somehow known but never been able to name. With language came awareness, and with awareness came understanding. Behavior change would be the next natural step, but that was, by far, the hardest part.

"I need to set some rules for dating," I said, as Olivia and I power walked around the lake one Saturday morning.

"What do you mean?"

I stopped to tie my shoe, looking up at her as I answered. "You know, being intentional … like with limits, and boundaries."

"I have two rules," Olivia said. "No alcohol or sex on first dates."

"Those are my rules, too, but I get a big fat F for compliance."

Olivia laughed. "I'm not very good at following them either."

"Sometimes I feel like it would be easier to just stop dating."

"So why don't you?"

"I'm thinking about it. But not just yet. Because I have a date lined up for next week."

She rolled her eyes. "Details?"

"He's English. His name is Liam."

"Is that the one who's a math teacher?"

"No, it's—"

"That guy with four dogs?"

"No—"

"The banker who's been married three times?"

"No! I didn't tell you about this one. I just matched with him last night. He's a ski instructor."

"A *ski instructor?*" She gaped at me. "Did you tell him you hate snow?"

"I did. Then he wanted to know how I felt about paragliding."

"What did you say?"

"What do you think I said?"

"I'm sorry, but this guy doesn't sound like a great match for you. What's the pull?"

"I find him physically appealing. And …" My thoughts drifted off, remembering the raffish, masculine quality that showed through in all of his photos. The first thing I'd thought of when I saw his profile was a book I'd loved as a child, some illustrated tome about Paul Bunyan. Something about the height, the broad chest, the strong arms, visibly sculpted by manual labor, as opposed to the studied bulge of gym workouts and protein drinks. Liam's profile even included a picture of himself with an axe in his hand, standing next to a pile of wood and a tree stump.

"And?"

I recalled our first few exchanges. *I'm looking for a relationship,* he had written. *Based on honesty and mutual respect.*

I repeated this to Olivia. "Well, who isn't?" she said.

"Oh, come on," I said. "That's naïve. Lots of people aren't."

She gave me a little shove. "Cynic!"

"I'm not being cynical." I laughed, shoving her back. "I'm being realistic." And I was including myself in that category. I was also into honesty and mutual respect, but how many times had my demons interfered with those best intentions?

I told Liam to meet me at my favorite restaurant in Geneva, with its continental fusion menu, colorful abstract art, and jazzy background music. I waited for him out front and spotted him coming across the street. He hadn't noticed me yet, and so I allowed my eyes to scan his physique, noting how tough he seemed, with those confident strides, broad shoulders, head up, eyes narrowed.

I had reserved us a table, but he insisted we start at the bar. "I'm still deciding if this is going to go as far as dinner," he said. His tone was borderline rude, so I thought he was surely joking, but his expression was serious.

"I guess I better be on my best behavior then."

"Guess so," he answered, appraising me with his eyes, his expression opaque. This wasn't the way the mating dance was supposed to play out; I was expecting him to fawn over me, to which I would respond by laying the flirtation on thick. But I couldn't even tell if he found me attractive, and I wasn't sure of how to position myself.

When we were seated next to each other at the bar, I allowed myself to study him again, the breadth of his shoulders underneath the soft blue pullover, the muscular thighs that somehow flexed right through his jeans. We ordered gin and tonics, and he told me about his divorce, how his wife had taken everything from him—his house, his money, his confidence—and that it was only now, seven years later, that he was finally himself again. "She kicked me to the curb," he said, "like a poor old dog. She should have just had me euthanized. Would have been a lot quicker."

I laughed. "It sounds dramatic."

"It was," he said, a glum expression lingering on his face. "Remind me how long you've been divorced?"

I fished in my glass for a cucumber slice. "I'm not divorced, I'm separated."

"And you're out with me?" His expression went dark. "That's bigamy!"

"No, it's not," I said, but my voice tripped. *Was* this bigamy? I couldn't remember the definition. "But I already told you all this when we first exchanged. What exactly is the problem?"

He drummed his fingers on the bar; they were long and spatulate, the nails neatly trimmed. "I already learned the hard way to never get involved with someone who's still married."

"Well, I'm not, really. I've been separated for a year and a half."

We looked straight at each other, allowing our eyes to lock for a few long moments. His gaze was penetrating, and I focused on the golden center of his dark brown pupils. Before either of us blinked, he said, "Oh, what the hell." Then he gestured to the bartender for another round of drinks. "Shall we have them at the table?"

While we waited for the waiter to bring our drinks, Liam told me a little about his life in the mountains and his passion for skiing. Then he caught me off guard. "Enough about me. I want to hear about you."

I had interacted with so many men who expressed not one whit of curiosity; that he wanted to learn more about me was a turn on. I told him a little about growing up all over the world and had just told him about my books when the waiter came to the table with our gin and tonics and some menus.

We listened as he made a little speech, in broken English, about the various specialities of the evening.

Liam looked from the waiter to the menu, and back again. "The seafood dish," he said. "Do you recommend it?"

"It's superb, if you like slimy fish," the waiter said, his word choice gone awry in translation.

"We prefer slimy people, thanks," Liam replied without missing a beat, and I laughed so hard I thought I'd pee my pants right there at the table.

We settled on something that felt homey, comfortable, safe: vegetable soup, puréed into a thick, orange consistency that looked like sunrise in the white, wide-lipped bowls it was served in. They brought it with a basket of crusty bread, salted butter, and little dishes of garnitures: seeds, chives, cheese, croutons. It was so delicious we ordered seconds, and by then we had stopped speaking in words. It was enough to communicate in grunts of satisfaction, pleasure with each bite, a shared moment that was warm, tasty, wonderful.

CHAPTER SIXTEEN

New Delhi, India 1985

Summer of '85. Moving again.

We left Egypt for India, touching down in New Delhi just after my sixteenth birthday. The US Embassy was having a housing shortage, so they lodged us at the Maurya Sheraton until they designated our official residence. Because we were a family of five and there were only two to a room, my parents took one, my younger sister stayed in another with my older sister (who was a month away from starting college in the United States), and I, the middle child, had a room all to myself—and on another floor!

The Sheraton was home to the hottest discotheque in Delhi, the Gunghroo, which was also where the kids at my new school partied every weekend. With my own room and an account with room service paid for by the Embassy, I became the hostess of the Friday and Saturday night pre-parties, after which we all teetered down to dance until the wee hours.

The whole setup was fabulous!

As was the privacy, because I needed time and space to get rid of all that food I was ingesting. India had upgraded my PB&J binges to something more sumptuous—*chicken tikka masala, mattar paneer, biryani rice, naan,* and for dessert, double orders of *gulab jamun,* sweet balls of milk dough that I mashed in my mouth like a gumming baby before slurping down every drop of the sugary syrup left over in the bowl.

When I finished, I marched straight to the bathroom and threw it all back up. My throat burned from the regurgitated spice, but I didn't even think about the harm I was doing to my body. I was just relieved to get it out. And it wasn't like I wasn't getting *any* nutrients. Throwing up was an evening activity. I did my proper eating in the morning, starting with a pot of south Indian coffee, richly brewed and blended with sweet condensed milk, accompanied by *masala dosa,* a savory rice pancake stuffed with potatoes.

Room service delivered it at the same time every morning, and I felt like a celebrity, answering the door in my thick terry-cloth bathrobe, the hotel insignia on its lapel, when the bellhop wheeled it in. It was always the same young man, and he taught me to close my eyes and chant *Om Nama Shivaya,* a Hindu mantra. I did as instructed, feeling very worldly and spiritual, until one morning when my eyes were closed, he swooped in for a kiss.

"Stop it!"

"Sorry, madame, sorry! Please don't tell boss, madame!"

Of course, I wouldn't tell. I was the Embassy brat in the five-star hotel, and he was some poor guy struggling to make a living. That alone made me feel guilty, along with this knowledge that I would be blamed. *Why on earth would you let that person into your hotel room?*

But I didn't know how to stop interacting with him, how to change the boundary from open to closed. So I continued to let him wheel my breakfast in, continued to close my eyes and chant, though inside, my mind raced. I prayed he wouldn't try any funny business. And I doubled his tip, a tacit agreement—in my mind, at least—that I would pay him to not molest me.

Only many years later did I find out that *Om Nama Shivaya* was an "invitation" to know yourself better, to attend to your inner life. Wasn't that ironic, given all I did was the exact opposite (though I thought I was so sage, treating myself to my morning *dosa* and letting my body keep it, as though I was a benevolent jailer, allowing my prisoner to eat).

Since I wasn't ready to attend to my inner life (was I even aware I had one?) I went all out on attending to my outer life, constructing an image of someone entirely in control of herself.

Delhi had wonderful markets at Janpath and Sarogini Nagar, with their endless stalls heaped with factory discard apparel created with the Western shopper in mind. Everything was ridiculously inexpensive, so I bought things I would never have spent money on before—flamboyant harem pants, sequined T-shirts, bohemian cloaks, elegant gowns—transforming me into somewhat of a maverick. I experimented with makeup, lining my eyes with blue eyeliner and thick coats of mascara. My hair grew long and tangled, and even though I was naturally blonde, it no longer felt blonde *enough*, so I dumped bottles of peroxide into my shampoo. Before long, I looked wild, white blonde hair heaped on top of my head, showing up at school in a ball gown and tennis shoes, or a pantsuit and a turban. I felt like I knew who I was now, done up, made up, larger than life.

My school in Delhi was a haven. There were no cliques, no mean Britneys slithering through the hallways looking for prey. It was easy to make friends. Prior to Delhi, I thought of teachers as distant quasi-enemies, punitive, judgmental, and disinterested, but here, even the teachers were nice. Suzy Thompson was my favorite. She had frizzy hair and big glasses, and she smoked; we even bummed cigarettes from each other sometimes.

Ms. Thompson taught English, and she seemed to be genuinely interested in her students. She always complimented my writing, responding in great detail to the pieces I submitted. In one assignment, she asked us to use images to convey a feeling, without ever stating it explicitly. I described the orange tips of two cigarettes, glowing in the dusk, the plumes of smoke entangled before my eyes. I was trying to describe my love affair with smoking, but Ms. Thompson interpreted it as a passage about two postcoital lovers. She kept me after class to talk about it. "The scene is so sensual," she said. "You made the reader *feel* the lovers without ever describing them."

I did?

"I have to ask," she said, "but are you all set with birth control?"

It took a moment for me to realize she thought that passage was about *me*! I didn't clarify her misinterpretation; it made me feel sophisticated to have written something so beyond my own experience. I had done my fair share of making out, but nothing involving nudity or *genitals*. Yuck. That word still made me feel completely disgusting.

I poured myself into the next assignment, writing a story about being trapped in the stomach of a fish, who swallowed me up to save me from a shark. Salvation turned condemnation, roiling in the acid juice of decaying plankton, darkness.

The day after I turned it in, Ms. Thompson kept me after class. "Is everything OK?" she asked, her expression full of concern. At first, I was confused, and then I realized: stomach, acid digestion, the big callus on my knuckle. Had she guessed I was bulimic? I stuffed my hand in my pocket. "Yes. Why?"

"Your story … it's quite … dark. Do you feel depressed?"

Depressed? That word wasn't part of my vocabulary, though years later it would seem so obvious. Between the binging and purging, the alcohol abuse, and the chain smoking, I was clearly having a mental health crisis.

Before I could answer, she said, "I'm worried about you. I've spoken to Dr. Beck, and he'd like you to come see him." Dr. Beck was the school guidance counsellor. He had a casual, affable presence around the school. I had sat behind him one night at the school talent show, mesmerized by his ease with himself, the way he sat so relaxed, legs crossed so that his feet stuck out in the aisle, tapping in time, his face beaming with love, as his wife sang "Mr. Bojangles."

Sitting before him a few hours later, I thought of that moment. On his desk, there was a picture of her. Next to it was a photocopy of my story with a note in Ms. Thompson's handwriting scrawled on the top. I tried to see what it said, but Dr. Beck picked up the pages and glanced through them. "Are you depressed, kiddo?"

"Why is everyone asking me that?"

"Well, there are some pretty heavy themes in your story. It's quite bleak. Almost nihilistic."

I didn't even know what nihilistic meant, but I said, "Yeah, I wanted to write about the bleak world we live in."

"Tell me more," he said, squinting his eyes knowingly. I contemplated telling him about my phony homecoming victory; I still thought about it every single day, even though it would soon be a year since it happened. But I was still too ashamed to tell anyone, so I just shrugged. "I guess I don't have much more to say." We sat in silence for a few moments, and then he looked at his watch. "Let's call it a day. But why don't you come in tomorrow? Just to check in."

I started going to Dr. Beck's office a couple times a week. We mostly ended up talking about writing. I told him about Calamity Collision, but I didn't tell him about Rose or Mr. Mulcahy. *That* would be bleak, when there was so much to be happy about in Delhi.

Eventually, the Embassy found our family a house, in a neighborhood called Malcha Marg. It was only a mile or so from the Sheraton, which was officially my second home, because going to the discotheque was *everything*. It was the place I could let loose, be drunk, be sexy, get attention. I would dance with any guy that approached me ... until I started going out with the DJ of the Gunghroo!

Vikas was tall, handsome, and twenty-two years old, but he looked younger, and I told my parents he was eighteen. They had no reason to question this; he looked so boyish, and he was so polite, ringing the doorbell when he came to pick me up, asking my father what time he should have me home. Whatever the answer, Vikas stuck to it; he wouldn't deliver me home a minute late, even when I begged him to stay out longer, knowing my parents would already be asleep.

He took me out all over Delhi in his little white Fiat, to places I would have never discovered without him. We had brunch at the Gymkhana Club, a members-only institution where Delhi high society played tennis and cricket, but we also had tea and *jilebi* at truck stops. And then there were the dinners, the rich, heavy dinners, at lovely restaurants all over town, which I gobbled down and threw back up as soon as I got home.

That genre of date was always staid, because there was little alcohol involved. Vikas didn't even drink. But on weekends, after a night at the Gunghroo, beer flowing in my bloodstream, Vikas would stop the car in the dark spots between street lamps. He was an amazing kisser, nothing like that repulsive Dirk in Cairo, and I got all melted and warm, arching into him on the front seat of the car.

I *loved* making out with Vikas … until the alcohol, which had suspended all communication between my brain and my body, wore off. Then, when I noticed the heaviness of his breathing, the dampness of his body, I freaked out.

"Sweetie," he said, "I don't understand." And all I could do was cry and say I was sorry. I didn't understand either. I wanted to do all that stuff … until I suddenly didn't.

He never argued, but after those episodes I obsessed about breaking up with him: it was too much pressure, I felt trapped, I hated him. Until I got swept up again in his expressions of unfettered adoration. They were like a match, lighting some performative fire inside of me, compelling me to give him what I knew he craved, even though it was the opposite of what I wanted.

I stopped seeing Dr. Beck and stopped taking such care with my homework. Ms. Thompson took the lighter nature of my short stories as reassurance that the counselling had worked, that now I was fine. And I was, wasn't I?

✳

Through my relationship with Vikas, I met stars from the Delhi jet set: millionaires, models, fashion designers. Eventually, we broke up, because he didn't like the way I consorted with Sunil Khanna, a flamboyant thirty-something designer who was trying to make it big in Delhi. His brand was called Splendour, and he marketed his wares by regularly staging fashion shows and pop-ups (before pop-ups were a thing).

I was sad about losing Vikas … but not sad enough to choose him over a friendship with Sunil, who furnished me with extravagant outfits that epitomized the Splendour label: billowing pants made from purple parachute material; midriff baring jumpsuits, a spin on the traditional sari, made with reams of gold silk; black taffeta cocktail dresses that made the number I wore to homecoming in Cairo seem hickish. He wanted me to be his walking billboard, he said, and cast me in all of his fashion shows as well.

Sometimes I strutted solo, sometimes on the arms of the hunkiest men I had ever seen, flown in from Bombay to "blow up" Delhi, as Sunil liked to say. I loved slinking down the cat walk, performing for the crowd. I reminded myself of this anytime thoughts of Vikas came creeping back into my mind. Every time I went dancing at the Ghungroo, I saw him. He looked so handsome in the DJ box, and I felt his eyes on me as I danced under the disco ball. I told myself he missed me, but deep down I knew that expression: pity.

Vikas was not impressed by Sunil's lavish events, hosted in five-star hotels or in the homes of his millionaire friends. He thought I was compromising my own reputation, running around with crazy Sunil. I told him he was being unfair, while feeling grateful that he wasn't around to witness how Sunil screeched up to the front of my house and honked, to the irritation of my parents, until I tripped down the walkway in my heels, already tipsy from the gin I siphoned from their liquor cabinet. My parents also didn't approve, but they had stopped trying to reel me in. The tacit agreement was that as long as I got good grades, I could do what I wanted. And what I wanted was to cruise Delhi with Sunil, feeling cool each time he passed me his flask of whiskey, oblivious to our recklessness.

One evening, he took me to a party where the crowd was actually my age, high schoolers and young people in their first year of university. It was nerve-racking when I realized this. I had been acting as someone well beyond my years for all these months; how did a seventeen-year-old behave? How was I supposed to be?

But within minutes upon arriving, I relaxed. The host of the party, a bubbly girl named Divika, introduced me around. Everyone was friendly, and it was fun to chat about life with people my age. Homework. University applications. Senioritis. A young man named Uday introduced himself as Divika's cousin. He was already eighteen and would attend college in the United States come September, in Washington, DC. The conversation flowed easily, and it was fun to talk about the States, being American and all, though by now the life I led looked little like the life of an American teenager.

Then the beer ran out, and the host asked Uday if he would drive to the kiosk, just down the road, to pick up more. He said sure and turned to me. "Come with me? We can keep talking."

We chatted back and forth all the way to his car. He pulled slowly into the road, the lights of the kiosk glowing in the distance, just a two-minute drive. He pushed in a cassette tape—John Denver singing "Rocky Mountain High"—and this struck me as funny, so I laughed.

Then, Uday floored the gas, and the car shot up the road, past the kiosk, onto a busy street.

"Hey, where are we going? The kiosk is back there."

"Let's go for a drink first," he said, reaching over and squeezing my thigh. His mild, conversational tone had changed to something determined, and it hit me that I was in trouble.

"I don't want to go for a drink," I said, pushing his hand off my leg. "I want to go back to the party."

"Tease." He reached sideways for my face, grabbing me by the chin. The car swerved into oncoming traffic.

"Watch out!" I shouted, shaking free from his grip. For the first time that evening, I realized the strength in his stocky body. He was shorter than me but compact and muscular, and the horrible realization that he would easily overpower me flooded my senses.

"You know you want it," Uday said, his hand back on my leg. He tried to pull me closer to him on the seat, which was a single bench, but I slid all the way over to my door. "Don't do that," he said. "Come on, touch me." He let go of my leg and used that hand to unbuckle his belt.

"Take me back to the party, right now!" I said, trying to sound fierce, but I couldn't hide the fear in my voice.

"We'll go back when you finish what you started." His pants were undone, exposing his erect penis. I couldn't believe this was happening, and I yanked my hand away when he tried to pull it to his crotch. He punched me, backhand, his knuckles landing where my collarbone met my shoulder. Then he grabbed the neck of my shirt and yanked. It ripped at the shoulder seam. I heard it tear, and I pressed myself as hard as I could against the door.

Then he made a sharp right, almost hitting a man on a bicycle. He had turned down a residential street, and just like that, all the chaos and lights of the busy road were gone; there was no more traffic, no other people, just dust dancing wildly in the light beams from his car.

He put his hand back on my leg. "Sorry I hit you."

I was crying, tears streaming down my face. "Please, can't we just go back to the party? *Please.*"

He slowed the car, looking for a place to pull over, and without even knowing if it was locked, I yanked the door handle and pushed. The door opened, and I fell out onto the road.

"Hey!" He slammed on the brakes, but I took off running in the direction we came from. The door of the car was still open, and he drove backward. "Are you crazy? Get back in the car!"

The street was lined with big houses behind tall gates, labels of security companies prominently displayed. I was screaming at the top of my lungs, running up to the gates, trying to shake them open. "Please let me in!" I sobbed, but no one came at the first and second house, so I kept running, kept screaming, while Uday shouted, "Get back in the car, I'll take you to the party!" The third gate had black metal rungs, like prison bars, and I could see the guard seated on a chair at the front door.

"Help me! Please help me," I shrieked, shaking the gate as hard as I could. But instead of letting me in, he turned around and rang the doorbell of the house. Almost immediately it opened, and a man, maybe sixty years old, distinguished with grey hair and glasses, dressed in black silk pajamas, stepped out.

"What is it?" he called. "What do you want?"

"Please let me in, he's going to rape me," I sobbed, looking over my shoulder at Uday's car, stopped at an angle in the street, the passenger door still open. He got out of the car, leaving the engine running, and came toward me, an angry look on his face. "Stop this nonsense right now," Uday said. "Get in the car. I'll take you back to the party."

I shook the gate harder. "*Please*. Please let me in."

The man spoke to the guard in Hindi, then went back into the house, closing the door. I heard the bolt slide into place. And then Uday was there, in front of me. But before he could say another word, another car appeared, driving fast, high beams on, blinding us both. Uday held his arm to his eyes as he hurried back to his car. It jumped as he floored the gas, taking off down the road, the passenger door still wide open.

I was crying so hard I didn't realize the person approaching me was a woman until she took me by my forearms and made eye contact. "You're safe now; you're safe."

She and her companion told me their names, Astrid and Lars. They were Danish. They'd been finishing a late dinner on their patio when they heard the screams.

"We've been driving around until we found you," she said. "You are young. Are you a student? Do you go to the international school?"

I was still sobbing, more quietly, but I couldn't yet speak. I could only hiccup and nod.

"Suzy Thompson is a good friend of mine," she said. "You don't need to be afraid; we will take care of you. You know Suzy, yeah?" Astrid asked, leading me to the car. I nodded yes, a new layer of panic igniting my insides. Were they going to tell her about this? Already the shame had taken over.

She opened the door of the back seat. "Get in," she said. "It's OK."

"I lost my purse," I said, feeling broken and pathetic, with my ripped shirt and empty hands. While I stood there, hiccupping between sniffles, the Danes surveyed the area. But there was no purse to be found.

"Don't worry," they said. "The important thing is you are safe now."

"It has my keys. And my cigarettes," I whimpered, as though listing the contents would magically make it appear.

"We have lots of cigarettes," Astrid said. "Let's go home. I'll make us some coffee, and we can smoke cigarettes together and decide what to do next."

A few minutes later, I was stumbling through their house to the patio where they were when they first heard my screams. There was a candle already burning, but melted way down, the flame dangerously close to the table. *Fire hazard!* My mother's voice sounded in my ear. Something about that candle, and the realization that what they heard was terrifying enough to have them run from the house without even blowing it out, caused me to shake. Astrid led me to a chair, and I sat on it woodenly until Lars brought a blanket from inside the house and tucked it around my shoulders.

I was exhausted. And I was wired. It was the most terrible feeling. I could barely move, even though I was jumping out of my skin.

Somehow, a cup of coffee ended up in front of me, and Astrid started rolling cigarettes. Her fingers were dexterous, efficient, and her tongue appeared in tiny glimpses when she licked the glue of the paper. A little pile formed on the table, and Lars took three and lit them simultaneously, passing them around the table, their burning tips like flares.

They asked me what happened; I tried to explain but I couldn't get past when I agreed to go with Uday to buy beer. I had this image in my mind: the lights of the kiosk at the end of the road. It was the last thing I remembered from my old life.

The events of my new life, the one that began when the "nice" guy at the party attacked me, emanated from their imprint on all five senses. The sound of the engine's acceleration. The feeling of his hand on my thigh. The sight of his dick and his hands on the steering wheel. The smell of the dirt. The bars of the gate in my hands. The click of the bolt. The taste of my tears.

Lars asked if I'd like to call the police. The *police*? No! What would they think of me, an American girl with big blonde hair, a torn shirt, in a car with a boy I barely knew?

"How about your parents? Should we call them?"

"Please, no," I begged, my mind back to my lost purse with the key to my house, and the knowledge that I would have to wake them to get inside. "They'll be so upset. I can't do that to them."

"But surely they'll want to help you."

And surely that was true, but I didn't want help. I wanted secrecy. I wanted to deal with this on my own, independently. No way would I pull them into a Mulcahy repeat. Guilt had governed my life since the Mulcahy fallout. Tonight, with the Danes, my trauma shifted from the incident itself to trying to hide the incident. I begged them to not tell Ms. Thompson; I was sure it would get back to my parents if they did.

When the Danes drove me home a few hours later, we found Sunil pacing outside my gate, frantic. He had my purse.

"Where were you?" he shrieked, his eyes wild in a way I had never seen. "Uday said you tried to have sex with him!"

Sunil's voice was a cross between disgust and anger, and I was so taken aback, I was speechless. It had not occurred to me I'd have to defend myself to my friend. But Astrid and Lars rescued me for the second time that evening.

"Calm down!" Astrid scolded. "She's been through enough for one night!"

"This 'friend' of yours," Lars said, addressing Sunil in a firm, no nonsense tone, "is a would-be rapist. Give me his full name and address."

Sunil gulped and looked at his hands. "He isn't my friend, sir. I met him tonight, at the party."

It was horrible: the look on Sunil's face, the shake of his hands, the tremble in his voice, his wet eyes. I had never seen him act like a normal person; he always came off as drunk, over the top. Now, he had morphed into an actual sober adult. It was unbearable to have him see me like this, the opposite of a Splendour girl, my face caked with dried tears and makeup.

It was just after 3:00 a.m. when I let myself into the house. I went to the kitchen and made some tea, and then crept to my room, praying my parents wouldn't wake up. I peeled off my clothes; a bruise had already formed where Uday punched me, two blue marks, one next to the other, the shape of his knuckles. I climbed into bed and pulled the covers up to my chin. I tried to smoke, but my hand was shaking so violently. I stubbed out the cigarette and slid down the pillows until I was flat on my back, covers over my head. Fat tears ran down my cheeks, becoming warm pools in my ears. I went to the party as a girl who was playing "normal" seventeen-year-old, and I came home "that" girl again, the kind that gets molested, the kind no one would really vote for, the kind a man tried to rape.

The Uday drama was a setback, but I partied and purged it right out of my mind. The bruise on my collarbone was harder to do away with, but even that faded, and I plunged right back into my Splendour girl persona with a vengeance, living my life with the fervor of someone whose days were limited, because they were.

We were moving again, this time, to Jakarta, Indonesia.

Most people would see moving to Indonesia under the comfortable wing of the US government as the opportunity of a lifetime. But I was sad. Moving meant the loss of home. The loss of identity. In Jakarta, I had no one. I was no one. I would start college at Mount Holyoke in South Hadley, Massachusetts, in September, and leaving Delhi for Jakarta meant that during winter and summer breaks I'd be coming "home" to a place where I had no history. But I knew how to adapt; it was my greatest skill.

CHAPTER SEVENTEEN

Geneva, Switzerland 2017

In the first weeks of my relationship with Liam, I drank enough gin and tonics to fill a small swimming pool and behaved like an infatuated teenager, making out with him at the movies, in the park, in his car. Some nights were so intoxicating I could only remember them in flashes, like fragments of an erotic film: licking a creamy dessert from a shared spoon, our legs intertwined under the table, the feeling of weakness when I was pressed against him in the shadows of a building, my hands running over his smooth head, his tongue sweeping my mouth in a way that made me dizzy. The sensation of all these buried parts of myself coming back to life was so overwhelming that one night I actually fainted in his arms like the tragic heroine on the cover of a romance novel.

In spite of this, we did not immediately end up in bed together as had occurred with Victor, Nigel, and all the others. Liam lived ninety minutes away on a mountaintop, and we only spent our first night together more than a month after our first date, one weekend when Lorenzo was away with Tano. I took the train to the town at the base of Liam's mountain. He was waiting for me at the station, and we drove thirty minutes in a harrowing ascent to his tiny chalet—more like a log cabin—in the mountainside commune where he lived. His village was a strange mixture of elderly French farmers, holiday homes owned by posh English power couples who drove in from London twice a year, and "boys" from the industrial areas of northern England, Scotland, and Wales who somehow ended up becoming ski instructors, making extra money doing manual labor off-season.

I was carsick by the time we arrived, but Liam drew me a bath, and I soaked and calmed my stomach while he cooked. Then he came in, soaped me up, and fed me sips of wine. By the time the water cooled, I was much better. He wrapped me in his comfy old terry-cloth robe, scooped me into his arms, and stepped across the threshold into the bedroom. When all was said and done, it felt more like having crossed the threshold into a whole new dimension, one that I had never known, where my body was treated not as a means to an end, with perfunctory foreplay and uninspired squeezes of those cliché parts that men always went for, but rather as something holy, before which he genuflected, concerned only with my pleasure.

Between the rich Burgundy he liked to drink and the marijuana from a farmer down the road, the weekend passed as though in a dream. Back in Geneva, in my "real" life, the one where I worked constantly, it came back to me in sensual flashes: straddling Liam on the sofa while he guided my hips with his enormous, rough hands; the urgent feel of him behind me when he hiked my dress up while I was washing the dishes; my legs wrapped around his back in the pitch black of a rainy mountain night.

We spent every weekend I was free like this, and this rapt sexual attention was everything I had dreamed of in the loneliest moments of my marriage. It intoxicated both of us, and covered up the fact that we had nothing in common. And though Liam was all the good things I had first latched on to—fun, generous, sensual—another side had begun revealing itself, one snarly, irritable flash at a time.

"I need an adrenaline fix," he said one Saturday evening. "Let's go paragliding tomorrow."

"Are you kidding?"

"No, I'm as serious as a heart attack." Liam cut the seal off another bottle of wine as we spoke, a belligerent expression on his face. "What's the problem?"

I narrowed my eyes to assess his motivations. Was this a set up? He *knew* I would never go paragliding. The mere thought terrified me; we had talked about it several times since our first date. He pulled the cork from the bottle with a loud *pop!* at the same moment I decided to give him the benefit of the doubt. "Remember? I'm not really into—"

"*Right*." He cut me off. "I forgot you don't know how to have fun. I forget because I've never been with someone so unathletic."

His tone was mean, and I didn't answer; I was still getting acclimated to his extreme passive-aggression, and this sort of comment hurt. But after ignoring each other for a few minutes, we went back to acting all lovey-dovey, and I tried to just forget it. The next day he redeemed himself when we were having a drink on an outdoor terrace in a nearby town, and a deranged man positioned himself a few meters from our table, staring at me and waggling his tongue. Liam reached the guy in three strides, and I watched, mesmerized, as he hauled this creep down the sidewalk, telling him off and sending him on his way with a push.

"I wish I could meet someone like that," Olivia sighed, a few days later over breakfast. "So *manly*." She was still reeling from her latest dating drama, a Swiss banker who seemed so "perfect," until she found out he was married.

I debated telling her the other side of the story, how anything could set Liam off, and his lack of self-awareness—that maybe his mood swings had something to do with the many difficult relationships of his past—turned me off. He had a huge chip on his shoulder as victim of his ex-wife, his ex-boss, his ex-girlfriends. It was even how he positioned himself relative to inanimate objects. "Don't do this to me!" I heard him screaming one morning while I was still snoozing in bed. I ran to the living room, expecting to see him fighting off a deranged killer, but it was only Liam, armed with a remote control, at war with a staticky television.

But I wouldn't share this version of Liam with Olivia; not today. I didn't like complaining about him, aware now that the problem was less Liam than it was me sticking with him in spite of all the red flags. So much for focusing on what I thought of him versus what he thought of me. It was just so hard to make that shift, so I found different ways to rationalize putting up with his crotchety fractiousness.

But then something shifted, taking us both by surprise. I was again in the mountains for the weekend. We were lying in a state of postcoital bliss when my phone pinged. I shouldn't have looked at it, but I was always afraid it might be one of the kids. It wasn't. It was an email from the workshop organizers, saying that Alistair Grand was having some health problems and they would postpone the event until further notice.

"I'm so disappointed," I wailed. "I had been looking forward to meeting him for months."

"You got the hots for that guy?" Liam asked, reaching for his iPad and looking Alistair up on Google. "Good looking bloke."

I peered at the screen. "That photo is old. He must be in his seventies by now."

But Liam wasn't listening; he was focused on the screen, reading Alistair Grand's many accomplishments in a muttering tone. Then he said, "I've heard his books are overrated."

I ran my foot up and down his leg. "Are you jealous of Alistair Grand?" I was trying to be coy.

"Are you kidding me, woman?"

"No, I'm not kidding you," I said, and then for emphasis added, "*man*."

"I don't know why you're spending good money and time on that old geezer."

I sat up and looked at him. "Because I want to build my writing career. He's a *teacher*. It's important to me."

Liam threw back the covers and glared at me. "You're stuck in your brain. Constantly overthinking. Frankly, it bores me sometimes."

"You know what, Liam? You're a real dick." I stood up abruptly. "And it's so obvious that you're just insecure."

"*Me?*"

"Yes, *you.*"

We got into an argument that escalated like a wildfire, until we extinguished it in a fit of passionate fury. Then we carried on with our day, cooking together, taking a long walk, hand in hand. But I felt something shift inside me, as if all those mounting doubts got distilled into one potent feeling: *this feels wrong.*

At my next session with Dr. Invicta, I shared my doubts about Liam. "Whole weekends with him sometimes feel very long."

"Have you considered spending less time with him?"

"We already don't see each other that often. He would be disappointed."

"We need to understand why you continue to struggle with setting limits. If you feel that the relationship with Liam isn't right for you, what is preventing you from ending it?"

"Well, I know he acts that way because he feels *bad* about himself."

"Undoubtedly. But what does that have to do with you? What makes you loyal to someone who treats you that way? What do you fear will happen if you put an end to the relationship?"

I felt my belly tighten; behind my eyes was the scene, vivid, visceral: Liam arguing, Liam upset, Liam miserable. And it would be on me. The idea was enough to stop me from acting on it, though I wasn't able to articulate why.

"Do you see how you take a position against yourself?" Dr. Invicta said. "It's a regressive stance. Do you remember what we talked about? How children learn to accommodate their—"

"Yes, but Liam's not an abuser!" I snatched a tissue from the box and balled it up in my hand. "He's just a jerk sometimes."

"I'm only pointing out the dynamic, because it's a repetition. You carry on with men you don't want to be with to accommodate their desires. But what happens to you when you do that?"

We fell silent, looking at each other. I smoothed out the tissue and began shredding it into little pieces, thinking about what she'd said. So many situations, with so many men, over so many years of my life spun behind my eyes like the reels of a slot machine. It would be impossible to count the number of times I had gotten through situations I didn't want to be in with men, because it was simply easier to adapt than to say no.

Dr. Invicta broke the silence. "At some moment, you will have to decide when you want to stop repeating this pattern. It won't happen magically. It's going to require self-awareness and setting limits. It all goes back to boundaries."

Boundaries, I thought, as I walked home from the session. And if I wasn't able to practice them with Liam, the tenant business was giving me ample opportunity. There had been no more moans and groans of afternoon delight since I spoke to Agatha that day. Nevertheless, a build-up of irritations—clogs of hair in the sink, greasy splatters of fried food all over the stove top, lingerie drying on the shower curtain rod during my working hours—kept me on my toes. Their little acts of quotidian obliviousness took on intimate proportions when they weren't *our* acts of oblivion, and it forced me to get comfortable with addressing them. *Please see exhibit A; do you mind?*

Not that I couldn't do that at all with Liam; the ferociousness of my response to his attack about Alistair Grand had surprised both of us. The difference between the renters and Liam, though, was that the contract with the renters had been spelled out clearly at the beginning. They knew that if they didn't respect my wishes, I would ask them to leave. You couldn't really do that with a boyfriend.

Or could you?

CHAPTER EIGHTEEN

South Hadley, Massachusetts 1987

New Delhi, India, to South Hadley, Massachusetts, via Jakarta, Indonesia, was not an obvious trajectory for anyone. But for someone donning Splendour attire, a weird platinum bouffe, and an eighteen-going-on-thirty cigarette smoking posture, preppy western Massachusetts was another world. I felt completely out of place in this sea of wholesome New England girls with their bobbed hair and monogrammed polos.

And it wasn't just an appearances thing; my foreign upbringing was not really relatable to others, and I found it hard to explain who I was. But while the answer to where I was "from" was usually a conversation stopper, my history with Mr. Mulcahy was far more accessible. At Mount Holyoke, #MeToo conversations were already alive and well, just not officially as they would be thirty years later. There was a rape support group, and around campus were crisis buttons, illuminated with a blue light, to be pushed if a man attacked you on your way home.

Didn't matter where you were raised, all women shared the fear of assault.

We had emotional conversations about it in the common areas, drinking coffee, playing cards, comparing notes about everyone's history of trauma. What was once my heaviest secret was now more like an identity tag: *Kristin, 18, molested by her best friend's father for two years when she was a kid; assaulted by an acquaintance in New Delhi a few months ago.*

"It was awful!" I would say. "But I'm fine! What's the saying? Whatever doesn't kill you makes you stronger?"

I still didn't have the self-awareness to consider that chain smoking, binge drinking, and rampant bulimia were not exactly the definition of "fine." Nor did I consider the misnomer in referring to that as a chapter from "childhood," as if it were so long ago.

Within weeks of starting at Mount Holyoke, I had a core group of friends from my dorm, and I plunged into party mode with dangerous determination. Smoking, drinking, and looking for guys consumed most of my attention. I devoted what little was left to half-hearted efforts at studying. I did not understand that college was a place to discover myself, my intellectual interests, what inspired *me.* I saw it as an obligation I had to get through to prove to the world I was smart, and for that reason, I chose a major—politics—I thought would accomplish that aim.

If only I hadn't been so good at pretending; if only my unhappiness had been more apparent and a watchful adult had offered me guidance. Had they, though, I probably would have rejected it, determined as I was to find a boyfriend. And though being at an all-women's institution did not facilitate the hunt, within a month of arriving at Mount Holyoke, I had one.

I met Tommy one night when a group of us girls went to Amherst College looking for some action. We milled around campus, swigging from a flask of vodka, until we found a party. Robert Palmer's "Addicted to Love" poured out of the top floor of a frat house, and I led the girls up the fire escape to see what was going on.

Tommy was standing at the window, all six feet five of him, drinking a beer from a red plastic cup. If it surprised him to see me, he didn't let on, instead laughing and pulling me through, holding me in a bear hug, making way for the other girls to tumble in on their own.

I stayed over with him that night and learned what all the fuss about orgasms was about. At first, it scared me. What was he doing down there to create this tingle that made my legs go numb and heat rise through my belly all the way to my face?

Once I understood, I just wanted more.

From that moment on, we were inseparable. Well, as inseparable as possible within the context of the busy life of an Amherst College double-major honors student, who also was the star of the football team. He had a full life, and he became my full life.

"I love you, baby," he said, within weeks of our meeting. "You've got me hook, line, and sinker."

"And I love you," I sighed, pressing my body into his.

"I've never known anyone like you," he said. "You're independent, confident, cosmopolitan."

He had no idea how needy I really was, that I was slowly but surely pouring my entire identity into him. His attention was a drug; I craved it as I did cigarettes, and sex took up all the space in my mind: the only time I felt certain that he loved me was when we were doing it. I relied on his reaction—the way he gazed at me through drunken eyelids, the way he devoured every inch of my body—to feel good about myself at all.

Despite my protests, my parents forced me to spend the six-week winter break in Jakarta with them. I sulked around the house the entire time, wearing Tommy's sweatshirt, complaining that I had to spend time in balmy Indonesia when I could be in the grey slush of Boston with him. Dad paid little attention, but Mom got mad. "You're boy crazy! Is Tommy all you care about?"

"As a matter of fact, yes!" I screamed. "And I can't believe you and Dad don't even care how this is affecting me to be away from him! I am not coming back here this summer!"

I was serious. I didn't want to be in Jakarta, where I didn't know anyone. I wanted to be like a normal American teenager, one that didn't have to be thousands of miles across the world from her boyfriend. "I'm staying in the States this summer, and you can't stop me."

"Where will you live?" Mom sounded exasperated. "Dad won't agree for you to just gallivant around the country."

"I'm going to get a job. In a grocery store. Or an ice cream shop. Like a *normal* person."

"When you can work at the Embassy? That would look far more impressive on a resume."

But I didn't care about impressing anyone but Tommy, and I bugged my parents relentlessly until they agreed that if I found a job that would allow me to pay my rent and food for the summer, they would let me stay in America.

When I got back to the States, I spent hours at the career center poring through binders looking for jobs in Boston, a mission that occupied so much time that I didn't really consider the way my relationship with Tommy was changing.

Now, when I called his room, the phone rang and rang, and he never answered. Some afternoons I spent hours pressing re-dial, tormented by the ringing, telling myself that if I let it ring sixteen times, he'd answer. Twenty times. Three rings, three times in a row. *Fuck! Why didn't he answer?*

One night, he was unreachable all night long, and I pressed re-dial so late into the wee hours that when I finally spoke to him at lunchtime the following day (*"I was in the library, baby"*) he told me the whole frat house was driven crazy by the incessant ringing, and I really needed to stop doing that.

"It wasn't me!" I was indignant. "I have better things to do than call you all night long!"

Which was, of course, a total lie. How could I have better things to do when the only thing I cared about was my relationship with him? Without Tommy, I was nothing, and the less connected I felt to him, the less connected I felt to anything about my life. He *was* my life, but I would show him. I couldn't wait for summer. I just had to find a job so we could live together. Then I wouldn't have to be constantly tracking him down.

I was thinking about this on the bus to Amherst one night. Thinking about it, hard, even though final exams started in a week and what I really needed to be thinking about was how to catch up with all the studying I had foregone in my quest to snap Tommy back to attention.

He was waiting for me, and as I stepped off the bus, he started laughing his head off.

"What's so funny?" Being greeted like this really irritated me, and I didn't hold back on showing it.

"You should have seen yourself," he said, still chuckling away. "I could see you when the bus was all the way up there." He pointed to the spot where the bus turned from the main road onto this quiet college street. "Oooh boy, you looked mad!"

"I'm not mad!" I said, unable to remove the anger from my voice.

And he was still bloody laughing!

I watched him have his little fit of hilarity, and then the bus driver said, "You two getting on?"

Impulsively, I did something I had never done, not once in the nine months I'd known Tommy: I got back on the bus, unrecognizable to myself as I did. And before I could change my mind, the door closed with that weird asthmatic sound, and the bus pulled away from the curb.

"Come on, baby," he shouted, running alongside my window. "Don't be like that." I stared straight ahead. He could work for my attention for once, dammit. The bus would get to the next stop in roughly two minutes, and I knew Tommy would keep up with it, fit as he was. I'd get off then and go home with him.

But when the doors wheezed open ninety seconds later, he wasn't standing there waiting for me. I looked both ways, and even stepped off the bus just to make sure there wasn't some blind spot hiding him, but he really wasn't there. He hadn't run after me. My heart dropped.

Why had I gotten so mad? Why had I played hardball? I should have just let him laugh at me; what difference did it make? Now, as the bus lumbered through the dark back to Mount Holyoke, I yearned for the safety of his presence, yearned to belong again to our relationship.

When I walked through the doors of the dorm twenty minutes later, I was relieved to see Kate in the TV room, watching *The Cosby Show*. She was a fellow cigarette smoker, so I knew her better than most. And she never looked rested, or freshly pressed, like so many of my dorm mates did, leaving for class with springs in their steps at 8:00 a.m. Kate sometimes stayed in her pajamas for days in a row, eating Pop-Tarts in the TV room, missing all her classes.

"Hey, woman," she said. "Are you OK? You look upset."

I gave her a basic sketch of what happened as I lit a cigarette, and she listened with big eyes. "I should get to my room," I said, stubbing out my cigarette. "Tommy's probably calling me right now."

"Can I talk to you about something?" Kate said, standing up and coming toward me. "Tommy is cheating on you."

"What do you mean?"

"Cheating. Like *crazy* cheating on you. He's slept with at least six girls behind your back. Two from Mount Holyoke, that I know of."

She grabbed my forearms as I shook my head. "*No.*" My eyes were wild, darting from her face to the ashtray, where the butt I had just stubbed out sat crumpled in the ashes. "I don't understand what you're telling me."

Kate tightened her grip on my arms. "*Cheating*. Seeing other girls. Behind your back. Having *sex* with them."

Suddenly all the weird behavior made sense, and oh God, I could not believe how dumb I was. I sank to the floor. It had never crossed my mind, never, ever, not even once, that Tommy was *cheating*.

Cheating?

Wait, what? *Cheating?*

I had trusted him so completely; cheating wasn't even a concept in my mind.

Devastated. Devastating. Devastation.

I felt my sanity collapse, like an eroded cliff dropping into the sea. "This can't be happening," I said, over and over, keening for all that had been washed away, taken from me in the riptide. Sense of place, belonging, identity, security—*gone.*

But even so, I wasn't thinking it was *over* between us. That would leave me with no place in the world anymore, nowhere to belong, figuratively and literally. Tommy begged my forgiveness, and I commanded myself to get over it so that I could still live with him that summer and we could be in love again. But then he dumped me anyway. He wasn't ready for such a serious relationship, he said.

Devastated.

Bereft about my whole stupid life, I couldn't stand the sight of myself any longer. I took a pair of scissors—*snip snip snip*—and my platinum locks fell in silky tufts to the floor. This provided approximately three minutes of distraction from the pain. I didn't know what to do, how to *be* in this horrible new reality. I needed a map, a compass, something to tell me how to navigate this hostile land. My existence was predicated on Tommy the football star loving me, and I was overwhelmed by his betrayal and the wrenching confirmation that there was something truly wrong with me.

And there was. Chlamydia, gonorrhea, and pubic lice, Tommy's thoughtful parting gift. When my parents got the bill from the Mount Holyoke Medical Center, they ordered me back to Jakarta. I was despondent; everything hurt, but I showed up at the dinner table with my parents, and to my boring embassy job, with a chipper smile on my face.

I'm fine!

Back at school sophomore year, completely depressed, yearning for Tommy, I cultivated my don't-give-a-fuck attitude, earning my reputation as the wild child of the party, the one always up for drinking and rounding up men, leaving a trail of one-night stands behind me like breadcrumbs. If I'd had my wits about me, maybe I'd have admitted how terrible I felt after these drunken liaisons with near perfect strangers, some nice young men, some not. Being wanted trumped everything: my hopes, my fears, my desires (did I even know what I desired?), my safety. I would give guys anything they wanted in exchange for some attention, and I acted like I was up for anything because that way, no matter what happened, it would look like I was the one calling the shots.

When alcohol and men were not available, I pulled sober antics, like streaking across campus while my friend drove the getaway car. I was a junkie for the adrenaline of laughter and cold air on my naked flesh, while campus police made pseudo gestures of trying to catch me, slow as possible, to enjoy the show.

One night, when a group of us were up late studying for midterms, I took off all of my clothes and climbed into the empty ice chest of the dorm kitchen. The other girls were in hysterics, wheeling me out the door and across campus, the naked queen on ice.

Later, back at the dorm, an innocent glance at the notebook my roommate had left open on her bed sent me into a tailspin:

Kristin masks her pain with debauchery.

I didn't even know what that word meant, but when I looked it up, I felt exposed, ashamed, *devastated.* I had never thought of it this way; in fact, I had never thought much at all about what had happened to me, how I had become, but when I saw those words in blue ink, bleeding into the soft grain of the page, some partial understanding of how completely fucked up I was clicked into place. The men, the booze, the smoking, the streaking, the non-stop hilarity … the throwing up. Oh God, did she know about that? It was the thing I was more ashamed of than anything; it was the thing that I knew gave me away for the sad person I was.

The cigarettes were a crutch I could not be divested of, but overnight, I stopped the rest: drinking, purging, running around naked, having sex. I wanted to redeem myself as a staid human being. But relinquishing my disguise felt as though my skin had been peeled off, exposing my nerve endings, and it hurt to be alive. One evening, I wandered out to the common area for a cigarette. I had spent the afternoon in my room, crying about everything, and nothing, I didn't even know. I found the German exchange student who lived on my floor weeping in front of the television. The Berlin Wall was coming down, the TV broadcasting footage of people tearing at it with their bare hands. In that moment, awareness of the larger world zoomed into my vision field, and I yearned to cry for something outside of myself.

A friend who was majoring in poetry invited me to a reading that evening, given by Mount Holyoke professor and poet Mary Jo Salter. I went along, as I did to most things like this, with the secret hope that there would be some amazing guy at the event who would fill the void Tommy had left. The pickings were slim, given that I was at an all-women's college, but there were always a few men that appeared from Amherst, Hampshire, or UMass.

But I forgot all about that fantasy when Professor Salter started reading from her latest book of poems. Her words were melodic, incisive, and I closed my eyes to listen, moved to tears by some long-ago memory of being read to as a child. When I opened them again, I watched the audience. People were rapt; some had also closed their eyes while Professor Salter read, some had their gaze fixed on her, slight smiles on their lips as they silently repeated her words.

Afterward, students called out to her as they left the room, "See you in class tomorrow!"

"You can take a class with her?"

My friend looked at me like I was daft. "Uh, *yes*. This is college. She's a professor."

I laughed; it was such a dumb question, but I was just excited. It was early enough in the semester that people were still adding and dropping classes. I got out of yet another boring politics seminar and signed up for a creative writing class with Professor Salter.

✳

Professor Salter was thoughtful, deep, and she spoke in a vocabulary that was so rich, so inviting, and yet accessible, words I knew already but never incorporated into my speech, or even my thoughts. It made me reflect on my stories, about the cigarettes, the fish belly, Calamity Collision, and further still, to a poem I had written in first grade that my mother had loved so much she'd taped it to the fridge: *I used to be a watch; now I am a tick.*

I thought a lot about how I used to be, and all the things that happened to me. Mulcahy. Britney. Dirk. Uday. Tommy. My self-image had taken a beating these years.

I used to be drunk all the time; now I am stone-cold sober.

I had wasted so much time at Mount Holyoke, trying to appear all intellectual and politically minded.

I used to mask my pain with debauchery; now I just hurt.

The class was a balm, something to look forward to every week. Our final assignment was worth fifty percent of our grade. I wrote a story about an orphan girl growing up in Gaffney, South Carolina, a place I'd read about in some magazine on some airplane headed to someplace; there had been so many flights to so many places, I had no idea. But I had remembered the details about Gaffney, population 12,000, the peach capital of America, the closest thing to small town USA I could fathom. The poor girl lived with her rich grandparents on their peach farm, and was so lonely and sad, until she befriended a farmhand named Charlie.

He was a lovely, caring man, fatherly and kind, and he let her hitch rides on the back of the tractor, and played cards with her on his lunch break. One day, while she was down at the creek, a masked man appeared. They struggled, but he was much stronger, and he raped her. She didn't tell anyone, except Charlie. She swore him to secrecy, but he went to her grandparents—*we gotta catch this guy!*—who blamed him for the crime.

She never saw Charlie again.

The title was "Someone's Gotta Pay."

I sobbed as I typed the last line, the injustice of what happened to Charlie unbearable. And I sobbed for the girl in the story; for her loneliness and despair, and her utter powerlessness at the hands of the adults.

A few days after I turned it in, Professor Salter left a note in my mailbox: *Please drop by during my office hours.*

I felt stressed. Did she think my story was pathetic?

A friend pointed out that maybe, just maybe, she *liked* my story, and why was I always so pessimistic?

But I was unconvinced and still holding my breath when I knocked on Professor Salter's door. "Come in," she called out, her voice friendly. When I stepped into the office, she said, "Have a seat. I've been wanting to speak with you since I read your story."

She combed through a stack of papers and then swivelled back toward me. I took the paper from her hand. At the top of the page, she had scrawled an A in red ink.

"This is a powerful piece of writing," she said. "May I ask if it's based on your own life? Do you need support?"

I was so relieved I sank back into the chair. "No, it's not true. I made it up." My voice cracked at the end of my sentence, and for a moment I yearned to tell her the truth. It was only then I allowed myself to feel the catharsis of telling the story of my loss. It was only then that I realized it was the first time in a long time that I had allowed myself to think about Rose.

Professor Salter looked at me just a moment too long, but she didn't press, instead saying, "If you agree, I'd like to use it as a teaching piece for the class. The writing is so vivid. I think it should be shared."

Her words—the approval, the recognition—thrilled me. Of course, I agreed. At that moment, as in class a few days later, I felt a sense of belonging. Validity. Esteem. And I realized, until I forgot again, caught up in the tumult of my life, that I had found my place. And it wasn't a country.

It wasn't with a man.

It was in language, paper, and ink.

CHAPTER NINETEEN

Geneva, Switzerland 2018

I leaned my forehead against the window and watched the mountainous landscape of Switzerland give way to Burgundy, France, with its hay-colored fields and hills dotted with cows lazily grazing. It was a beautiful afternoon in early spring. The air outside was crisp, but they had turned off the heat in the train, so I pulled my arms inside my oversized sweater and hugged myself.

The workshop was finally happening, six months later than it was originally scheduled. Alistair Grand had sent out an email to all the participants himself, apologizing for his long convalescence—apparently, he'd had multiple complications following a hip replacement surgery—and telling us to come prepared with specific goals. This matched my mindset perfectly; all I did anymore was set goals, it seemed. There were so many things to plan for now that I was managing my own life. But Alistair Grand obviously wasn't asking about whether I had set up that retirement fund yet (I had) or whether I had learned how to do my own taxes (I hadn't, but I had made a decision to hire that task out).

My writing goals were two. First, I needed to start writing again. I had managed to submit fifty pages before the original deadline, but had made little progress since, despite all the time that had passed. Second, I needed to figure out the ending.

These goals were linked. I blamed the slow advance on Liam—*He's so demanding! He takes up all my free time!*—but the problem was me. I couldn't quite find the way to write about the difficulties I had being authentic with men while I was in a relationship with a man I wasn't being fully authentic with. History was repeating itself, as Dr. Invicta kept reminding me, but I gave myself grace: I couldn't change overnight, and at least with Liam, I was learning to fight back.

The conductor came through the car, and I dug in my computer bag for my ticket. When I handed it to him, he asked if I was a tourist. I almost nodded yes, but caught myself and gestured at my computer bag. "*Non, je suis écrivain.*" I'm a writer.

I felt shy about trying on this title; I was so used to sandwiching it in between all the other things I called myself, or apologizing for having self-published my first two books as though they didn't count. But the conductor didn't blink, and we chatted for a few minutes about the workshop. Then he moved on, examining tickets and making small talk with other passengers.

I turned back to the window. I'M A WRITER blinked in my mind like a neon sign, and then my thoughts segued to something I had not thought about for years: Calamity Collision. Good old Calamity. Abidjan felt like a million years ago, and yet, like yesterday. I smiled, remembering how Rose and I thought Judy Blume would bring our dreams to life. Was I projecting the same hopes onto Alistair Grand?

I was still bruised from that agent's comments that my story was unimportant, a dime-a-dozen anecdote. What if Alistair Grand reacted the same way? More than ever, I believed that what Mr. Mulcahy—and the State Department—did needed to be added to the growing heap of #MeToo literature, but that didn't mean others would agree. And then there was the writing itself. The pages I submitted were in the second person voice, and though Dr. Invicta thought it was wonderful, I couldn't discount that transference-countertransference element of our relationship. Were we playing mama and daughter? Would she admire anything I produced?

With the rhythmic *clack-clack-clack* of the train lulling me, I drifted off, clutching my computer, thinking about how a year earlier, I was only just making sense of the fact that I had been so childish with money and life planning. Now, here I was, fifty pages into a new book and attending a workshop that I had paid for all by myself. I had this sudden and overwhelming urge to call Tano to say, "Look how far I've come! Look how well I'm doing!" I wasn't gloating; I wanted to tell him of my progress, wanted him to be proud of me. But I resisted the urge. He had his own pain about our split; it was unreasonable to think he would cheer me on as I grew up and away from our marriage. But this awareness couldn't take away the yearning for his approval.

The workshop took place in a beautiful old farmhouse outside of Dijon. Brambles of wildflowers crept up the old stone, giving to tangles of vine just past the flower garden, where spring blossoms sat in bright, unruly rows. Every detail was so imperfectly perfect that were I not there in person, I might even say it was fake, a painting of what someone imagined an idyllic house in the French countryside should look like.

Participants were lodged in tiny cabins scattered around the property, far enough from the main house for privacy, but not so far as to feel unsafe. Of course, not everyone would feel unsafe if tasked with spending a night in the countryside by themselves, but I was not one of them. Being braver was a lifetime goal that had so far eluded me. Alone in the dark, the innocent stirring of a harmless animal or the rustling of the trees was enough to put my heart into overdrive.

The event kicked off that evening with a group dinner and wine tasting. We were eight total, plus Alistair Grand, who, in person, was much smaller than I had imagined. True, I had seen him in person all those years ago at Mount Holyoke, but I had been in the audience, and he on a stage behind a podium. Since then, the same black-and-white portrait that graced all of his back covers had shaped my image of him. It was both disappointing and reassuring to discover that he was life-sized and so very human, limping along with a cane, a stain on his shirt and a flake of dried blood on his cheek, some accident of shaving that he hadn't noticed or hadn't cared enough about to clean.

The participants were all women, and Alistair Grand made a few comments about his great fortune at being holed up for the week with eight lovely ladies. We all laughed, though the woman next to me also muttered, "Here we go!" I glanced at her, but she kept her eyes glued to the front of the room. Later, though, when the second bottle of wine was being presented, she whispered, "You know he has a reputation?"

I wondered what she meant. Surely, *he* wasn't a womanizer, though my assessment was prejudiced. Just because he had that same pasty skin and Weeble-Wobble-esque shape that reminded me, I hated to say, of Mr. Mulcahy, didn't mean he wasn't popular with the ladies. There were so many unattractive but wealthy men with beautiful female counterparts. Money was men's currency, and beauty was women's.

In the afternoons, Alistair would teach. But mornings were for writing, or the ninety-minute one-on-one tutorial session with him that was part of the package. I had been looking forward to this ever since I signed up. The morning of my session, I walked through the wet grass to the cabana where tutorials were held. It was a simple wooden structure made of varnished pine, with a floor and ceiling but no walls, though it didn't matter; it was far enough from the main house and the other cabins to give a sense of privacy.

Alistair was already seated at the wooden table placed there for the occasion, and I watched him watch me cross the grass toward him. When I got closer, he raised his hand in greeting.

"Hi!" I called, as I climbed the three steps to enter. "I've been looking forward to our meeting!"

"Sit." He gestured at the chair across from him. There was a pitcher of water on the table, and he poured us each a glass. "Why second person?"

I was taken aback by the question. I knew we would discuss it but hadn't imagined it to be the first thing he'd say. That old, shaky place inside me rumbled to life. "It's … it's the dissociative voice?" I stumbled over my words, trying to channel Dr. Invicta's, while fighting that voice that lived in my head. *No one cares about your stupid story.*

He grimaced and waved his hand for me to stop talking. Then he reached into a battered leather case on the floor next to his chair and pulled out a plain yellow folder. In it were my pages. "Put it in first person."

I started to speak, but he cut me off.

"You have that flair," he said, "to run toward, not away from, danger. And this is essential for good writing."

It wasn't the first time I had heard this, though never approvingly, never to suggest it was a bonus to my oft-dreamed of writing career. Rather, I had heard it from past therapists, who called it counterphobia. *Your subconscious mind drives you toward 'dangerous' situations that allow you to re-enact past traumas. It's a repetition compulsion.*

"But you've got to put it in first person," Alistair's voice cut into my thoughts. "Otherwise, the story won't work."

He sat back in his chair, as if to say, *you gonna fight me on this?* I looked him in the eye. They were a watery blue color, with heavy, drooping lids. *Basset hound eyes.* Both of my grandparents had them, and now my father did, too. In a few years, I'd be next in line.

"Can you tell me why? I'd like to understand—"

"Because you're asking the reader to become *you*. And that makes for a hard read, if you're telling the story of the molestation. Anyone who reads your book will have done so because they want to know about *you*. How *you* dealt with it. How it affected *you*, and *your* ability to have relationships with men." He cleared his throat and sipped some water. "And if the reader is 'you,' where are *you*, actually? Where are *you* hiding? Voice matters, my dear."

Later, I sat in my bed with my laptop, my mood switching from contrarian to discouraged to resigned, and back again. Alistair Grand said that voice mattered, and I hadn't paid all this money to ignore the teacher's advice, which boiled down to one principal fact: I couldn't tell the story *and* stay hidden behind the second-person voice. My true self needed to narrate.

I felt him come up behind me and slip his hand past the waistband of my shorts.

My face blazed as I wrote. I felt as though I was being lifted into another dimension, one without enough oxygen. Kaleidoscopic scenes twisted to life inside my head: Mr. Mulcahy, my parents, my humiliation, my regret.

I closed the computer and went to the bathroom, where I stared at myself in the mirror, buzzing with adrenaline. Then I splashed my face with cold, fresh water. *Breathe.* Back at my computer I drafted an email to Alistair, arguing with his directives, telling him about Winnicott's true and false selves, explaining my rationale for telling my story in the second person. When I read through the message fifteen minutes later, it sounded dramatic and incoherent. I deleted it and started over. "Thanks for the tutorial this morning. I think I didn't explain ..."

I stared out the window, unsure of how to complete the sentence. What didn't I explain?

Alistair Grand's opinion was in service of the eventual reader. He had no idea that his editorial vision aligned perfectly with the major theme of my post marital transformation. How I dealt with the question of voice and the shame that had split me in two was the final frontier, and it occurred to me, as I stared at my own words on the screen, that the only way out was to own it: this is what happened to *me*.

On the last night of the workshop, at the pre-dinner drinks, I ordered a glass of white wine at the bar and made my way to Alistair. He was standing by the fireplace, chatting with some of the other participants. When they eventually drifted off, he asked me, "How's the writing?"

"Well, I took your advice."

"Good. And?"

"It's hard."

"And?" His tone suggested that I was stating the obvious.

"And nothing. I'm working on it. I don't know if I'll manage to pull it off—"

He rolled his eyes. "Another writer with imposter syndrome! Welcome to the club."

"You've felt that way?"

"Still do! And I'm about to turn seventy-five; I'm working on shaking it by eighty." He raised his glass to mine. *Salut!* Then he took a long swallow. "Let's keep in touch. You can send me pages. I'll mark them up for you. Help you get oriented to the new voice. Pro-bono," he added.

"That's extremely kind of you," I said, taken aback by his offer. "Are you sure?"

"I wouldn't have offered if I wasn't sure. And I'm not promising to edit the whole book. I don't think you're ready for that anyway, not with only fifty pages written. But I'm happy to take you on as a mentee."

"I'm so grateful," I said. "How will I repay you?"

"You can give me credit in the acknowledgments when it becomes a bestseller. And I'll be in Montreux in a couple of months for a wedding. That's near to Geneva, isn't it?"

"Yes. Less than ninety minutes by train.

"Then it's settled. You can take me out for a drink then."

Later that night, Alistair Grand regaled us by reading from his work in progress, and we shared last glasses of wine around the fire. Oddly, I felt that same mix of exhilaration and fear I'd felt when Tano and I first separated. Five days earlier, I hadn't known how the workshop would go, how my writing would be received. The feedback ran far deeper than just some editorial suggestions, and it had pushed me to grow .... and here I was, still standing. I had been afraid of my story for so long, and now something had shifted.

I felt brave.

CHAPTER TWENTY

Seattle, Washington, 1991

The summer I graduated from Mount Holyoke College, my parents moved from Jakarta to Lagos, Nigeria. More than ever, I yearned to put down some roots, to have a solid base to call home. None of the countries I had lived in with my parents were an option, nor was there a base in the USA to go back to. I needed to carve one out for myself. So I signed up to be a VISTA volunteer in Seattle. VISTA—Volunteers in Service to America—was the domestic Peace Corps, something I thought would be the perfect job since I didn't want to go back overseas.

I was assigned to an agency that helped pregnant teenagers, and I could hardly wait to get busy. I wanted to help people. But my enthusiasm was quickly dashed; the agency didn't provide direct services to teens, it wrote policy. It might have been a chance to use my writing skills, but they had nothing for me to do, though expected me to be there eight hours a day, idle. I spent my time hiding out on the roof to smoke cigarettes and chatting with Kenny, the therapist down the hall, whose office I had to pass each time I crept out for a smoke. Kenny walked with a limp and wore a boot with a two-inch platform, to compensate for the height differential after his leg was crushed in a horrific car crash two years earlier.

At first, I just popped my head in. *Hellooo!* I liked to say, something funny before I launched into whatever one-liner I had about the "nightmare of my life" that day. I had taken to using this expression to define most everything I talked about.

"How come everything is always a nightmare?" Kenny asked one day, stroking his scraggly blond beard with his left hand. His right hand squeezed a ball, more physical therapy after the crash.

The question caught me off guard; no one had ever asked me to substantiate what I actually meant. "Just joking!" I said, pirouetting down the hallway.

"Hey, hey," he called, coming to the door of his office. "Not so fast. I'm genuinely interested."

"Really," I said, feeling put on the spot. "It's just an expression."

"Which you use an awful lot. Maybe you're trying to pass a message?"

I knew that if I said I wasn't, it would only look defensive. As I was contemplating this, Kenny said, "I just get the impression that you don't want people to know you."

This hurt in the way my roommate's journal entry about my debauchery had, and I would not let him be right. So, I accepted his invitation to come back after my smoke break to continue the conversation. By the time I left his office an hour later, I was seriously rethinking my compulsive use of "this is the nightmare of my life." And Kenny had extended a drop-in policy to me: if his door was open, that meant he was free.

I started wandering down there throughout the day, grateful to escape the tedium of my job. Naïve to the rules of therapy, I gave no thought to the lack of structure around these meetings: there was no fee, no time parameters, no rules against the long hug he gave me when I arrived, and again when I left.

It was like another Dr. Beck, although Kenny wasn't really fatherly. He was more like someone's weird older brother that burned incense and wore cool political T-shirts. And talking to him did help. I felt acknowledged, like he was genuinely interested in me, and I found myself thinking about what I would tell him next. But ever since I started telling him stuff about myself, I also felt anxious, like I had gotten on a runaway train. I had a weird feeling in my body. Emotion was close to the surface; I felt like I might burst into tears at any moment, all the time.

And what were Kenny and I talking about?

Mr. Mulcahy.

I told him everything: how it started, how it blew up, how the State Department dismissed it as an unfortunate little blip. By the end of my story, his mouth was hanging open. The State Department protected a pedophile? This was institutional collusion! Institutional betrayal! He asked for more details, of which I had few. He wanted to speak to my parents, and like a good girl, I said yes, even though the very thought caused my heart to clench up like a fist. What could he possibly tell them that would not carry us all back to those terrible and dramatic days in 1982?

He told me not to worry; it was a practical matter of wanting to be compensated for these therapy sessions. But it was also a legal matter: the State Department should foot the bill.

Conveniently, my parents were on their way to the United States from Nigeria, and I agreed to give them his number. It was the first time since the whole drama blew up nine years earlier that I had been open to discussing it with them.

But after their phone call with Kenny, my mother reported that he asked for a list of the typical vegetation in the Ivory Coast.

"*What?*"

"He wants to re-create a tropical environment. Or something like that. He sounded like he knows what he's doing," Mom said, though she sounded dubious. "It's to help you get connected to that traumatized part of yourself."

"*Traumatized?*" The concept itself was traumatic. "He said I'm *traumatized?*"

"He said when you talk about … *it* …" She said the word as if it burned her mouth. "It's like you're talking about someone else. As if it isn't a story about *you*. He called it disassociation."

I wanted to kill Kenny. He had already spoken to me about disassociation; how this thing I referred to as "getting through" was actually a response to trauma. That not only had I disconnected from my feelings about what happened to me in Abidjan, I had also disconnected from my body. Surely that was how I "got through" all those episodes with Mr. Mulcahy, he said, but now it was working against me because it suppressed my instinct to protect myself.

"It's counterphobia," he said. "It's compulsive. You run straight into dangerous situations."

Whatever it was, I didn't want to discuss it with my parents! I knew I should never have agreed to this. My mind was filled with images of Mr. Hornsby, Dr. Feare, and my parents completely freaking out. If I was "traumatized" by anything, it was the fact that everyone else had been so traumatized. I was not about to put anyone through *that* again. I told my mother I had to get off the phone, and I stumbled to the kitchen to splash water on my face. Anxiety washed through me, wave after wave. And then, outside of the window, who did I see? Kenny! I had given him my address for the correspondence he was preparing for the State Department, but I had not expected him to show up like this. He was standing in the driveway, squinting at the windows of my split-unit building, trying to figure out which one was mine. I dropped to the floor and crawled from the kitchen to the hallway, where there were no windows.

I waited there for at least ten minutes, biting my hand so hard I left teeth marks. Then I crept out on tiptoes, irrationally terrified of finding him sitting in the kitchen. Only when I noticed the envelope taped to the window of the front door did I exhale.

It was the letter he'd drafted to the State Department, detailing the events as I had explained them, and demanding restitution. It was exactly as we had discussed, but I suddenly had cold feet. It's not that I didn't want some money. After a year of being on the measly VISTA stipend, I was broke. But I was feeling cornered by Kenny, trapped by him. I kept thinking of that manila folder on his desk with my name on it, and all the things I told him. I felt embarrassed. Ashamed. Disgusting.

All at once, I kind of hated him, and the thought of facing him became unbearable.

Back at work, he confronted me. "You're acting like you don't want me to know you again."

I feigned surprise. "I wonder why you think that?"

He shot me a look: I had caught him at his own therapist's game. I stopped going to his office to chat, and I took a different route to the roof for my cigarette breaks. And boy, did I take a lot of them. I must have been smoking two packs a day, anxious as I felt.

I quit my job. They had no use for me, and why was I reporting to that office every day when it meant facing the stress of seeing Kenny? Soon after I stopped going to work, he started calling me, and I spent weeks dodging his phone calls, paranoid that he would show up at my house again.

In the meantime, my parents returned to Nigeria, just as a scandal was unfurling in the Embassy community, casting a weird sense of déjà vu. A guard had been fired and reported to the local authorities for molesting the child of an Embassy family at the community swimming pool. The State Department stepped in to take care of the family, with psychological support and repatriation.

My mother detailed the situation in a letter: *And then I told them what happened to you, and how nothing was done at all to help. I told them about Kenny's letter. And they said you should get in touch with the office of tort claims at the State Department. They said they will help you pay for therapy.*

I could hardly believe it. Just like that, they wanted to help?

My mother's letter included all the relevant contact information, but I stalled on making the call. It felt daunting, calling up the State Department, who didn't give a shit about me, or any of us, when we most needed support. Mr. Mulcahy had been running free ever since Abidjan, and this alone made calling attention to myself even more terrifying. What if it got back to him? What if he tried contacting me to tell me to shut the fuck up? I could still see his eyes, bulging out. *Shhhh! This is our secret!*

I told myself that I could do it tomorrow. And when tomorrow came, I told myself the same thing. A few weeks went by. I got a job as a barista at a coffee shop. Kenny stopped calling. I started to feel safe again, and I pushed the tort claim out of my mind.

Thank God I quit that stupid VISTA job. Making coffee was so much more fun, bopping around behind the counter to the Indie rock radio that was always playing in the background. Peter Gabriel's "Solsbury Hill" was on all the stations that season, and whenever I heard the lyrics, I felt a swell of recognition. For the longest time, my heart had also been going *boom boom boom*, but it was only in this new calm that I could realize that.

No one I served coffee to had any reason to suspect how complicated my life was, and I liked it that way. No more *boom boom boom*. Now I was just the smiley girl behind the counter, and my interactions with the regulars, who greeted me by name and dropped coins in my tip jar, lent to a feeling of such normalcy, such happiness, I took on extra shifts and spent as many hours per day at the café as the schedule permitted.

One day, a young military officer came into the café wearing his fatigues. His name was Joseph, and he was an ROTC corporal who had just moved to Seattle. He wasn't a regular, but was forthright about his desire to become one—as long as it was me behind the counter, he said. I couldn't believe someone that good looking was interested in me. He was at least six feet two, well built, with the most beautiful golden skin. His face was boyish; he was quick to smile, and his brown eyes crinkled in the corners when he did. After several mornings where he sat at the table closest to the bar, flirting while I gave him free refills, he asked if I wanted to have dinner with him. "We could try out that new Italian place down on the waterfront," he said.

"I'd love to!" I jotted out my address, the buzz of possibility pulsing through me. Maybe he would be my new boyfriend! Maybe we'd fall in love! I hurried through the rest of my shift and raced home to shower and change before he picked me up.

Joseph showed up right on time, and I felt the frisson of romance when he ran around the front of the car to open my door. "You look great!" he said, giving me an approving once-over.

My hopes soared. I really felt the connection between us, and I beamed at him through the window as he ran back to the driver's side. As he climbed in the car, I said, "I can't wait to try this restaurant."

But he turned in the opposite direction of the waterfront. "I couldn't get a reservation for this evening, but they gave me one for tomorrow," he said. "Guess we'll just have to see each other twice in a row." He winked and added, "Tonight, I'm cooking for us."

My heart lurched. *This wasn't the plan. Should I say something? But that might offend him.* I tried to calm down by reminding myself of the facts: He was friendly. He wanted to cook for me. He wasn't aggressive. "Helplessly Hoping" was playing on the radio, and he sang along loudly. This reassured me somewhat. *A murderer wouldn't sing along to Crosby, Stills, Nash, and Young,* I told myself. But I was stressed and still trying to decide what to do when he suddenly pulled up to the curb.

"My palace," he said, gesturing to a red brick duplex. "I'm on the ground floor." He turned off the ignition and the music died. There were two guys playing frisbee on the lawn next door, and they watched us as we got out of the car.

"Hey, man," one of them called out, and Joseph raised his hand in salute. "You going to Mallory's later?"

"Haven't decided yet," Joseph answered. He introduced me to his neighbors, which also reassured me. *A murderer wouldn't introduce their victim to the neighbors.* They exchanged a few more words, and then we were at the front door, Joseph inserting the key into the lock.

The smell of garlic hit as soon as we entered the house. "Oh, yum," I said. "That smells wonderful."

"Garlic bread," he said, waving me into the living room. It was sparsely furnished, with a big leather couch and a television set sitting on a milk crate. Joseph picked up the remote and said, "The stereo is built in." A few seconds later, the first notes of Gregory Abbott's "Shake You Down" filled the room. Joseph pulled me toward him. "Dance with me."

His arms circled tight around my waist, and I put my hands around his neck. I wanted to be the type of girl who slow danced in the living room with a gorgeous guy. *This could be the beginning of something real,* I thought, my mind flashing ahead to some unknown future. I could see us together around a table with a bunch of friends, telling the story of how we met. I tried to not be nervous, even as I could feel his erection through his jeans, feel how hard he mashed his pelvis against mine as we swayed to the music.

"Hey, relax," he said. "You're tense." He massaged my waist, and then he was kissing my face, my neck, and finally, my lips, pushing his tongue into my mouth, moving it in time to the music.

I did not want this.

I wanted to be at the Italian restaurant on the waterfront.

I could hear the guys playing frisbee outside; they were still talking about Mallory's party. Joseph started working my pants down. I didn't help him, but I didn't say no. It felt impossible, alone here in the living room with him. If I protested, wouldn't he just force me? Later, I'd pinpoint this as the moment I went outside of myself, tossing my head back, acting like I was into it as he turned me around and pushed himself into me from behind. I was afraid I would topple forward, so I steadied myself by reaching behind to hold on to him. This excited him more, and he became frenzied, hammering away at my flesh. I squeezed my eyes closed, praying for it to be over. Behind my lids, all I could see were two dogs humping as his pelvis grew damp against my buttocks. He groaned, "Oh *fuck*. Fuck fuck FUUUUCK."

Then, in staccato, he twitched and shuddered, and everything down there went soft and drippy. Outside, the conversation was still about Mallory. *She's so cool, man.*

Semen ran down my leg. I tried to catch it with my hand, and instead caught sight of my jeans, sagged around my ankles. I yanked them up, giving up on trying to prevent his body fluids from getting on my clothes.

Joseph used his T-shirt to wipe the sweat off his face. Then he went to the kitchen, whistling. "Wanna beer?"

Through the door, I watched him open a bottle and take a long swig. He saw me looking at him and said, "Cheers," holding out his bottle in invitation.

"Where's the bathroom?" I asked, and he pointed down the hallway.

I felt like I was moving through gelatin: my senses coated, my legs heavy. I reached the bathroom as Joseph turned up the music. R.E.M. belted "Stand." I locked the door and stood there for a few seconds, then I sat on the toilet and tried to expel whatever of him remained inside me. I could smell his saliva on my face.

I must have been sitting there for a few minutes because suddenly the song changed. Sinead O'Connor wailed "Nothing Compares to U," and I cried a little. Then he shouted, "Dinner!" and I pulled myself together and joined him in the kitchen. He had prepared a pot of spaghetti, and dumped a jar of store-bought sauce on top of it, where it sat, solid but collapsing in cold, red chunks. There was a loaf of garlic bread, store-bought and perfectly sliced, sitting in its aluminium baking wrapper. It looked like he had already eaten half the loaf. Now he was twirling pasta on his fork, the sauce splashing his shirt, like a spray of blood.

Afterwards, he wanted to go to Mallory's, and I agreed, just to get the show on the road. As soon as we were out of the house, I said, "Actually, I'm not feeling great. I think I'm getting my period."

Joseph put a protective arm around my shoulder. "I've got a hot water bottle. You want to just stay in and watch television? I don't mind—"

"It's fine. Really. I think I just need to sleep it off." I held my breath. I just wanted to go home.

"As you wish, fair lady," he said, opening the car door for me. When he turned the key in the ignition, the radio came on. Elton John sang "Tiny Dancer," and I stared out the window while Joseph hummed along. Ten minutes later he kissed me goodbye at the door. "I'll call you tomorrow," he said, and I nodded, all cheerful and smiley.

Inside, I locked the front door and listened to the sound of his wheels pulling away from the curb. Then I locked myself in my bedroom and lay in bed, chain smoking all night long, watching the red numbers on the digital clock change, waves of humiliation crashing against my insides. All I could think about was the sight of my jeans around my ankles.

Suddenly, it was 6:00 a.m.; time to get up for work. I hadn't slept at all. Cigarette butts filled the diet Coke can next to my bed, and in the shower, when the water hit my head, smoke literally rose from my hair. The small bathroom became a chamber of fumes and steam, and in that moment, I despised myself, scratching at my flesh, shampooing my scalp so hard strands of hair came out, sticking in sad tendrils to my fingers.

I called in sick and got back into bed with a can of diet Coke and more cigarettes. I lay there for hours, staring at the ceiling and smoking, getting up only to pee. I just couldn't sleep, even as I craved the comfort of unconsciousness.

The phone rang, once, twice, three times, and then the machine picked it up. Joseph's voice filled the room.

"Hey there, you OK? It must have been pretty bad for you to take off work today! I got you some flowers and had to give them to some dude at the counter! Kidding! I'll give them to you tonight. The reservation is for 7:30, so I'll come by around 7:00, OK? Call me."

When he hung up, I lit another cigarette. I felt crazy. Was I being a drama queen, getting all stressed out about last night? Should I go with him tonight?

Dragging myself out of bed, I stood before my closet, where a single blouse hung lopsided on the hanger. My chest was tight, I felt breathless ... oh my God, was I having a heart attack?

I stumbled to the bathroom and splashed cold water on my face, over and over, until even my hair was wet. Then I stood before the mirror and slicked my hair back, rivulets of water running down my face like tears. I probed myself for information: was my heart beating normally? I didn't really know how to take my pulse, but I tried, holding my fingers to that blue line snaking through the underbelly of my forearm. I started counting beats—*boom boom boom*. Was a heart supposed to beat that fast? All of this was my fault, smoking like a bloody maniac.

Boom boom boom!

I called 911. "I think there might be something wrong with me," I said, my tongue thick and dry in my mouth. "I think I might be having a heart attack." Then I started crying, so hard I could hardly answer the questions the male operator asked.

He transferred me to a female officer, and I told her what happened, though the narrative was not entirely coherent. I was caught between the two stories that played out in parallel last night. In Joseph's version, he took me home for dinner, and I let him fuck me, and it was just great for both of us. In my version, we made a plan to go to a restaurant, but he changed the plan and didn't tell me until I was already in the car, and I tried to be cool because I wanted him to like me, and the second we got to his house, he made the moves and I was afraid if I didn't play along, he'd force me, and technically, he really didn't, but it felt like he did.

The officer was kind; she called me sweetheart and assured me that what I was having was more likely a panic attack than a heart attack. She told me I needed to go to the Sexual Assault Center, at Harborview Medical Center, and helped me figure out the bus route. Somehow, I made it over there.

A therapist named Janet received me, and her sympathy, her seriousness, and her use of the word "rape," transported me back to that night in Abidjan, when my father told the houseboy that Mr. Mulcahy had raped me with his finger. There, in Janet's office, I had no strength left, and no weight, either, nothing to tether me anymore to the here, the now. I was whirling so fast in this vortex of anguish I feared I might come apart in a million little pieces.

But with Janet in charge, I somehow got calm enough to tell her everything that had happened. She said, "Let's reset your boundary first." We talked about what I would say to make sure Joseph didn't come by my house that evening, or ever. Then she dialed the number, passed me the receiver, and watched me, leaning forward, her eyes big, brown and doe-like.

With Janet next to me, I was prepared to speak to him directly, but his machine answered, thank God. I left a message saying I had got back together with my boyfriend and to please not contact me ever again. I would have given anything for this to be true, for some wonderful protective man to actually be the reason Joseph had to stay away from me. I didn't believe that what *I* wanted held any clout.

When I hung up the phone, Janet said, "How do you feel?"

"Guilty." I blew my nose. "Anxious and guilty."

If my answer surprised her, she didn't let on. "Of?"

"Well, if he thought it was such a great time, I'm sure he feels bad now. And what must he think of me?"

"Let's focus on what you think of him," Janet said.

But I had started crying again; I couldn't think about anything. Janet showed me some breathing exercises, and made me tea, with sugar, to stabilize the lightheaded feeling that came from not eating all day. She asked me what I did, generally speaking, to take care of myself.

I told her I'd have to think about it and get back to her.

CHAPTER TWENTY-ONE

Geneva, Switzerland 2018

What do you mean, you need time to work on your book? We haven't seen each other for two weeks!"

Liam was upset. He had driven into Geneva so we could have dinner together and talk over the squabble we'd been having—about spending time together—ever since I got back from the retreat ten days earlier.

"I just have so little time to work on it during the week, so I have to prioritize it on the weekends. Please try to understand."

He sulked and poured himself the rest of the wine. He had already drunk the majority of the bottle. "When will *we* see each other?"

"What do you call this?"

"You know what I mean. Like a real couple who spends real time together."

"I just want to get some traction with the manuscript. Alistair Grand has offered to help me, and I don't want to keep him waiting."

"So you put that old codger before me!"

"No! I'm putting *me* before you! He's doing me a huge favor. I'm afraid if I don't send him some pages soon, he'll forget his offer. Please try and understand."

"Have you considered that I might forget my offer?" Liam scowled.

"What offer?"

"You know what I mean!"

Before I could answer he nodded his chin to a nearby table. "Look at that."

I followed his eyes to a young woman dressed all in black, a skin-tight skirt and sweater set that showed every voluptuous curve. She was partially turned toward us, her long blonde hair blown into elaborate bouncy curls, her red lipstick a perfect match to the red stilettos donning her feet.

"*She's* got a great figure." His eyes practically licked her. "Why don't *you* dress feminine like that? You'd be much more attractive if you did yourself up a bit. Heels, makeup, style your hair, maybe a bit of running to tone up your legs and fanny?" He pushed his plate back and gestured for the waiter to bring another bottle. Then he leaned back in his chair, stretched, and tried, unsuccessfully, to suppress a belch.

I was speechless. Had he looked at his own outfit? Buttons straining at the belly of his shirt, high waisted jeans, a throwback to another era entirely. I wouldn't have been surprised to discover a wide-toothed comb in his back pocket.

The waiter appeared with the menus and Liam said, "I'm not that hungry. Shall we just share a pizza?" I nodded, my face tingling with anger. "And another one of these," he said, waving the empty bottle of rosé.

As the waiter walked off, Liam reached for my hand. I yanked it away.

"Come on," he pleaded. "Don't be like that."

"Like what?" I said coldly.

"*That*," he said. "You *know*."

"I didn't appreciate your little speech. Or your lecherous gawking."

"I'm sorry." He sounded defeated. "I wanted to hurt you. I'm upset that you don't seem to care whether you see me or not."

"Do you really think it makes me want to spend time with you when you speak to me that way? Or when I see you drooling over someone young enough to be your child?"

"Erase what I said from your mind. It was idiotic. I don't know what came over me. Except, you know …" he laughed, nervously. "*Wine.*" He put his hands on the table, palms up, as if asking me to take them, but I didn't budge. "You want to know what the worst thing is?" Liam spoke quickly, as though he was making a sales pitch. "I've been thinking about some things you've been talking to me about. You know, #MeToo and all."

"What does that have to do with it?"

"You said you're trying to take care of yourself. Well, I want to take care of you too." The waiter brought the wine and we fell silent as he topped up our glasses. When he walked away, Liam continued. "Talking with you has opened my eyes. I'd never thought about all the things you women go through. And I've come up with an idea. I think you're going to love it."

I gestured for him to tell me.

"I've decided to form a 'League of Gentlemen.'"

"What does that mean?"

He looked excited. "Society needs a registry of good guys, men that women can feel safe with. A bloke wouldn't be able to become a member of the League of Gentlemen without a first-hand recommendation from a woman."

I should have acknowledged how refreshing it was to hear a man spontaneously express care for all the violence women have to deal with, and to think proactively of a solution. Instead, I said, "That would never work."

"Of course, it would!" He still looked so enthusiastic. "Think about it. The *only* way for a man to become a member is by direct nomination. He'll *have* to be vouched for!"

"But it would never work!"

"Hear me out!"

"I'm sure Larry Nassar's wife thought he was just wonderful."

"The point?"

"Abusive men aren't abusive all the time. There wouldn't be any way to vet the 'truth.'"

Liam's expression changed as this information landed. I hated the fact that I was right. I wished his idea could work. Were it possible, it might even end violence against women, or at least drastically reduce it.

Just then the waiter brought our pizza, and we didn't go back to the conversation. Liam spoke jovially of other matters, and I could tell he was nervous that I was still upset. I was, but now I felt sorry for him, so I tried to calm the tension by smiling along to his banter. Why was I so afraid to hold on to my anger? Why was I so afraid to disappoint him? I couldn't quite explain it, but I knew that the situation was intrinsically related to the dilemma of my manuscript: the voice I needed to tell my story was the voice I would need to end this relationship once and for all.

A few days later, I told Dr. Invicta about the dinner with Liam. "I was so close to ending it right then and there."

"So why didn't you?"

"In the last year I have learned so much about myself and the unhealthy way I relate to men. I've gotten much better with setting limits and standing up for myself. And even though I still sometimes *feel* stuck when I think about breaking up with Liam, I know that I'm not. I know my feelings aren't the facts. But it's hard."

"What's hard?"

Silence came over the room as her question landed. Even the cars outside the window seemed to stop. I felt sweat prickle to the surface of my hairline. "The hard thing is that disappointment factor. I've been thinking about this a lot ... I ... I ... just can't bear to disappoint him."

"I want to ask you something."

I nodded, but Dr. Invicta waited another long moment before speaking. "How is it that you see men?"

"What do you mean?"

"How do you *see* men?" She spoke slowly, watching my face.

"I don't get what you're asking me."

She leaned forward, looking straight into my eyes. "How do you see men?"

"I don't know!" I laughed uncomfortably. "What do you want me to say? They're men!" She didn't break eye contact, but she didn't say another word, so I continued. "I see men as … males. Adults. Men!"

"And if they're the adults, what are you?"

I suddenly felt exhausted. I closed my eyes; I just needed a minute.

Then the penny dropped: I saw men as adults.

The adults.

And I saw myself as a child.

"I think there's a young girl still living inside you," Dr. Invicta said softly. "And I think she believes she has no choice, that she has to do what the adults say, or risk their anger, or worse, their disappointment."

Time froze, and then it shifted, as some dreaded sensation pushed against my mightiest effort to hold it at bay. I knew who Dr. Invicta was talking about; that young girl was still there, locked in the bathroom, barely breathing, terrified of the rattle of the door handle.

"I want to talk to that girl," Dr. Invicta pressed, her voice calm, measured, the way you'd speak to a scared animal. "I want to ask her if she knows she is important too?"

I was sobbing before I even realized it, great heaving cries coming from some deep chamber inside me. "I should never have told."

"Why?" Dr. Invicta said. "Why should you have to protect a grown man?"

"Because I ruined everything."

"What did you ruin?"

"Everyone's happiness. My parents' happiness. Rose's life …" My voice trailed off, overwhelmed by memory. I trembled, and Dr. Invicta handed me a soft blanket from the basket by the couch.

"Put this around your shoulders," she said. "You're releasing trauma; you need to stay warm."

My teeth chattered. "I'm scared."

"What are you scared of?"

"Of getting in trouble," I whispered.

"Getting in trouble for what?"

"For not obeying."

Tears dripped down my face in a steady stream. I wasn't even sure who was crying: The young girl who lived in fear of getting in trouble? Or the woman who lived with constant sorrow for this child?

CHAPTER TWENTY-TWO

Seattle, Washington 1992

I didn't go back to the coffee shop job; I was too afraid Joseph would come in. But I was broke, and meeting with Janet twice a week, so with her encouragement, I called the State Department office of tort claims. The man I spoke to explained that a tort claim covered the costs of damage incurred by the plaintiff, and the State Department was prepared to cut me a check for $20,000. Accepting their offer meant I wouldn't bother them again with this matter.

In my mind's eye, $20,000 was a *huge* sum of money. This was 1992. My stipend as a VISTA volunteer had been a measly $500 dollars per month, and though working at the coffeeshop had been better financially, it still wasn't great. Minimum wage was $4.25, and though I was paid $6.50 an hour, after rent, expenses, and groceries, there was nothing left over. I could hardly believe my good fortune. Twenty thousand dollars! It was like being offered the winning lottery ticket. I agreed, and he posted me the papers that very day.

It was a surprisingly simple document: one page on which I had to print out exactly what Mr. Mulcahy did to me, and then quantify, to the best of my ability, each act. What an embarrassing task this was, sitting there with Janet trying to calculate episodes of getting molested by Mr. Mulcahy. It was like advanced multiplication: If there were so many weeks in a year, and so many days in a week, and if the abuse started roughly this date and ended roughly that date, how many episodes of buttock pinching were there? How many for "digital penetration"? Could I quantify the impression of an erection? Did the sounds of icky breathing, the smell of sour breath, also get counted?

I kept thinking about how many women had filed this sort of report before me. And how many had never gotten to file any report at all because they weren't believed, or their abuser had killed them?

I reflected on this to Janet. "I feel like what happened to me isn't bad enough to deserve all that money."

"Not bad enough?" Janet looked at me like I was crazy. "How can you say that?"

"Well, it's not like he raped me," I said, my mind flashing to that long ago night when my parents learned the truth. *He raped her with his finger!*

Janet put down her calculator. "That man did a *terrible* thing to you."

"But—"

"There is no 'but.' Mr. Mulcahy victimized you, as did the institution that protected him. *Period.* Women endure horrible things at the hands of men, and that one person may have gotten it 'worse' does not mean that what happened to you is any less terrible."

I mailed the claim back to the State Department, and started looking for a job. It would have been easy to get a position in another coffee shop, but I needed a change. When a case worker position at a local shelter for street kids opened, I applied, though I didn't really have the qualifications. My decision to apply anyway, on the last day the position was open, was so last minute I had to drop the application off by hand. A woman with purple hair who looked old enough to be my mother skimmed my application and said, "Thanks for applying, honey!"

"I'm actually not really qualified."

"Says who?" She smiled over her horn-rimmed classes. "Why don't we go straight to the source?" She shouted over her shoulder, "Malcolm! Yoo-hoo! Malcolm!"

A handsome, thirty-something man with George Michael stubble, wearing a T-shirt that said FAG in big letters across the chest, came to the front desk. I stood there feeling ridiculous and hopeful as he skimmed my application. Then he looked at me. "You're right, this position requires someone with an MSW or equivalent. But there is another position on the outreach team you'd be qualified for. Why don't you apply for that?"

My new job as an outreach worker for street kids gave me the sense of purpose I had hoped to find as a VISTA volunteer. There was no sitting around with nothing to do; every shift was action driven, from getting meals on the table at the drop-in center to doing intake interviews, which quickly became my favorite task. I told Janet all about the kids I saw and how good it was for my spirits to feel helpful.

"What you've been through has given you a capacity to empathize with emotional hardship." She smiled. "Maybe someday you'll become a therapist."

It was the first time I had ever considered that meaning and purpose might come from the difficult things I'd been through. I felt affirmed by Janet's suggestion that I could someday play the role she played for me. I began using our sessions to talk about some kids I interacted with until one day she commented on it. "We seem to talk a lot about other people."

"Well, I'm just so upset by their stories. Sometimes I can't even eat, I'm so upset."

Janet probed deeper until I admitted I sometimes exaggerated for dramatic effect.

"But why?" Janet asked.

"I don't know," I shrugged. "For sympathy?"

"But if you get sympathy for something that didn't even happen to you, does it actually help?"

It sounded absurd when she said it out loud, so I laughed. But she was not going to let it go so easily.

"Do you see that you're playing a role?" Janet studied me from across the room. "I think you're being who you think *I* want you to be. Which puts you in the position of having to relate to me in a way that isn't authentic."

"I don't know," I said, looking out the window. "Are you saying I'm not really concerned about those kids?"

"I know you are a humane and sensitive person," Janet said. "But I also know that you don't let me know where you really need support."

"That's not true; think of the day we met!"

"That was a crisis. I'm talking about day to day. You don't let me know who you really are."

My mind flashed to Kenny. *You don't want people to know you.* I had been so incensed when he suggested that. *Me? I'm an open book!* But if I was honest with myself, what I let others know about me was highly curated. I kept all the self-doubt and yearning to be loved hidden behind my cheerful mask.

"Are you aware of it when you slip into a role with me?" Janet said.

I shifted uncomfortably. "I don't know."

"Sometimes I think you tell me stories about something other than what is really bothering you."

"Why would I do that?" I sounded defensive, but I couldn't help it. It was embarrassing to have what I said picked apart this way.

"I don't know; that's why I want to talk about it. I imagine you want a response, but have trouble asking for it. So, you tell me stories to get some attention that is probably similar to where you really need attention. And what I'm asking you to do is try to tell me how *you* feel."

I looked away from her. I had been telling people what I thought they wanted to hear for so long, I wasn't even sure I knew what was true and what was false.

"I'm going to ask you directly. What do you *actually* want some sympathy for?"

I wanted to answer, but it was impossible to articulate. How could you ask for sympathy if you couldn't even explain where it hurt?

"Maybe the child inside you yearns for some acknowledgment that you were wronged, first by Mr. Mulcahy, and then by the State Department?"

"The child inside?" I scoffed. "I don't think that's it."

"I want you to do something," Janet said. "When you're out in public, at the grocery store, or the lake, look around. Look for kids ten, eleven, twelve. Look at them and note how *young* they really are. Let yourself remember you were that age, too."

I walked home that day, contemplating this assignment, thinking I might even jumpstart it en route. But it was the middle of the school day, and the only kids I saw were sound asleep in baby carriers and strollers. I was ambivalent, anyway. If it were even true that there was some inner child floating around inside me, I didn't want to get in touch with her again. Even thinking about it took me right back to standing before that mirror once upon a time, willing my body to be different. Wasn't therapy supposed to help me feel better about myself?

But the assignment vanished from my mind when I got home and discovered the $20,000 check from the United States Treasury in my mailbox.

Twenty thousand dollars!

The first thing I did was call Janet to tell her the money had arrived. She didn't answer, so I left a message on her voicemail. I was aware of how excited I sounded, and that I probably wasn't supposed to be rejoicing. But I couldn't help it: I'd struck gold!

And all I could think about was getting a pair of Doc Martens. I had been wanting those shoes ever since I got to Seattle. All the cool grungy girls wore them. But they were so expensive, I hadn't been able to buy myself any.

But now, $20,000!

I took the bus to Capitol Hill, the hip neighborhood of Seattle, where I did much of my outreach work. I didn't see anyone I knew when I went into the shoe store, but when I came out in my new black Docs, my old sneakers in the bin, I ran into some fellow outreach workers.

"Doing some shopping?" one of them said.

"Nah," I lied, feeling shy about sharing my excitement about these shoes. "Just browsing." We stood in a circle and chit-chatted for a few minutes, and I felt successful, like I was now officially part of the crowd.

I decided to walk back to the University District, but halfway down the hill I could not ignore the stiff heels of my transformative new shoes tearing into my flesh. God, it was painful, every step like a razor shaving back the skin of my heels. I could see the blood on my socks. I was too far down the hill to catch a bus, and too far from either neighbourhood to find a store to buy some Band-Aids. I finally took off my shoes and socks and walked barefoot until I reached the next bus stop. No one saw this, except unknown passers-by in cars, but I felt humiliated in front of myself.

When I got to the bus stop, there was a teenage boy listening to his Walkman; he ignored me, and for that I was grateful. I winced as I pulled my Docs back on, folding my socks into lumpy makeshift bandages, wedged painfully between my heel and the stiff leather. When the bus came, I had to buy a ticket, and I was aware that the sock on my left heel had slipped out of place and was hanging off the back of my shoe.

"Miss," an old lady in priority seating called. "Your sock."

I tried to ignore her, but she kept saying it: *Miss, your sock! Miss, your sock!*

I limped down the aisle to a free seat, my face burning. I could feel heads turn as my dilemma got broadcast, loud and clear. *Miss, your sock!* It was ironic, I realized, as the bus pulled back into traffic: a micro version of public humiliation, nine years after the greatest public humiliation of my life, when the entire embassy community learned what Mr. Mulcahy had been doing to me. Maybe these blisters had erupted to remind me what those twenty-thousand bucks were for: *Justice.*

Not Doc Martens.

I rode the bus as close to my home as I could get, that word thrumming in my head. *Justice.*

Justice. Justice. Justice.

The bus left me on "the Ave," the vibrant main drag running through the neighborhood of the University of Washington. My sock-bandage must have fallen off somewhere between my seat and the door, because there was no trace of it anywhere on the sidewalk. Now I had no protection for those raw wounds, already staining the insides of my new shoes.

I gritted my teeth and started walking toward home, trying to control the pain with a mantra. One slicing step. *Justice.* Another slicing step. *Justice.*

Within minutes, the wounds won. I took off my shoes and continued barefoot, dodging dog poop and bits of broken glass all the way home.

CHAPTER TWENTY-THREE

Geneva, Switzerland 2018

You never told me about the payoff." Dr. Invicta said.

"It wasn't a payoff. It was 'compensation.'" I laughed, but it came out more like a bark. *"Twenty thousand!"* I said, in a sardonic, auctioneer's voice. *"Do I hear twenty thousand? The price for a girl's body!"*

I looked past Dr. Invicta to the painting on the wall. It was a beach scene: children playing with sand buckets, a calm ocean in the backdrop. I'd never really paid attention to it before, and now it made me think of Grand Bassam and that ten-year-old girl in a Snoopy bathing suit who had been stripped of her innocence in a matter of minutes.

Abruptly, I changed the subject. "I'm taking Krav Maga lessons."

"Krav Maga?"

"It's a self-defense technique—"

"I know what it is," Dr. Invicta said. "I didn't know you were interested in that sort of thing."

"I saw an ad for it on Facebook. Fifty percent off. Lessons for two people. I was going to do it with Carmen, but we didn't get around to it, and I only have a week to use it before it expires. I'm going to take Lorenzo instead."

I hadn't told him this yet, and I was pretty sure he would absolutely hate the idea.

I was right.

"Mom! No way!" Lorenzo threw himself face down on the sofa when I told him about the Krav Maga lessons.

"Think about Agatha and Ursula."

He froze. "*They're taking lessons too?*"

"No. But I want to remind you of how you dreaded having renters. And it turned out OK, didn't it?"

He started to protest, and I said, "Remember what you said?"

Both Ursula and Agatha had recently told us they were moving out. Ursula was moving to New York, and Agatha was being sent to Haiti on a six-month mission. Lorenzo said he wished they weren't leaving—not because he had fallen in love with the arrangement, but because he had gotten used to them, specifically.

"Yeah," he said, looking glum. "I also said I didn't want them to leave because now we have to start all over again. And imagine if we get some weirdo."

I tousled his hair. "If that happens, we'll be happy we know Krav Maga."

"Mom! It's not funny!"

"I know it sucks to start over with new people. But we can do it. We know how. And I promise I won't let any weirdo move in here."

"But how will you know?"

I thought about it for a minute. "I guess I'll have to trust my instinct. And that worked pretty well with Agatha and Ursula."

He nodded.

"And you know, I'm going to take my time choosing someone. In fact, we don't even need to have two tenants anymore. I'm earning enough that we only need one. And how about we wait until next month to start searching? We can go for a few weeks without the extra income." I felt a rush of pride that I was able to offer Lorenzo this reassurance.

His eyes lit up. "A few months?"

"Just a few weeks." I laughed. "But give me time. It's not always going to be like this. I promise you."

✳

The following evening, I dragged Lorenzo to the gym where we'd be learning Krav Maga.

"Do we have to do this, Mom?" Lorenzo's eyes were pleading, and I couldn't blame him. The place was grey and cold, filled with barbells, punching bags, and throngs of sweaty men leaping up and down and grunting.

"Come on," I said, taking his hand and pulling him toward the small group assembling in the corner. Lorenzo and I were the oldest and youngest of the group, and Lorenzo the only boy. The teacher, Benoit, was a powerhouse, a stocky man made of solid muscle who taught by scenario: a gun in your back at the cash machine, a group of men jumping you from behind late at night when you're walking home alone, a lone wolf lunging at you with a knife. We took turns attacking each other, while Benoit directed our maneuvers: forearm to block the punch, palm to the chin, push the face back while your knee goes to the balls … When he handed out foam daggers for the next drill, I lunged at Lorenzo, shrieking, "If you don't clean your room, I'm gonna kill ya!"

I thought it was hilarious, but Lorenzo kept a stone face, and when it was time to reverse the roles, he barely waved the knife in my direction.

"Come on!" I begged. "Give me a chance to practice getting attacked, too."

By the end of the lesson, I had lost my Krav Maga fervor. It was clear that to become dynamos of the streets, Lorenzo and I were going to need to take thousands and thousands of dollars' worth of classes. I knew Lorenzo, as a young man, was more at risk for stranger attacks.

But I knew that most attacks on us women weren't from random men. It was men we knew, and fighting them off physically wasn't always the sort of defense needed. It was protecting ourselves from all the emotional and societal manipulation we needed training in. Learning Krav Maga was like trying to escape a burning building by doing the polka.

A few weeks later, I helped Ursula and Agatha lug their bags down to the curb, where a taxi was waiting to take them to the airport. We hugged goodbye, and I waved until they were out of sight, thinking of how much had changed in my life in the year since they had moved in. I had survived the breakup with Tano. I had survived—so far— the world of middle-aged dating. I had written a good chunk of a new book. I had learned to be handy around the house and manage money.

I re-activated the Facebook ad for the vacant room and listened to the radio as I tidied it up. The top story that day was more #MeToo fodder: Donald Trump and his nominee to the Supreme Court, Brett Kavanaugh, both accused of sexual assault. My mind roamed to other recent high-profile stories: Dominique Strauss Kahn and his "aggravated-pimping" at the Carlton Hotel. The Stanford University swimmer-rapist, Brock Turner, appealing his conviction. Larry Nasser. Harvey Weinstein. Jeffrey Epstein.

And then there was William Mulcahy, whose story had been buried, paving the way for him to assault God only knows how many girls after Abidjan.

Mulcahy. Mulcahy. Mulcahy.

Mr. Mulcahy was all those men; and they, he: men who saw girls and women as objects, to be used for their own purposes. It was painful and enraging, the misogyny that blanketed society. And it was so difficult to decode, because not all men are abusers. But of all the abusers that exist, the large majority are men.

As my anger about this flared, so did my inspiration to write. Passages of my story emerged in short little bursts. I wrote in second person, turned them into first person, and sent them off to Alistair Grand. He always responded within hours, sending the pages back with thoughtful notes typed in the margins. He'd said he also had imposter syndrome, but it was hard to fathom. The way he used words turned the most mundane subject into something interesting. Every email that came in from him filled me with anticipation. I felt alive, tingling with hope as I opened his messages, hungry for the red of his track changes, hungry for his wisdom.

Soon other details of our lives crept into our messages: my marriage ending, his estrangement from his wife, my protectiveness of my children, his regret that he'd never had any, my dreams of becoming a writer, writing as his only outlet for emotional expression.

"I admire you for the work you do as a therapist," he wrote. *"And for what sounds like great closeness with your children and many friends. My only intimate relationship is with the blank page."*

I was thrilled by the deepening of this unexpected connection with Alistair Grand, and I thought about him all the time, between sessions, while cooking dinner, out walking around the lake. I felt like I was in love with him. Or maybe I just wanted to *be* him, to possess his facility with storytelling and not be afraid to write the truth of what had happened to me.

"And I admire you for your amazing body of work," I wrote. *"I don't know how you do it, where all that inspiration comes from."*

"You can thank yourself for anything I've written lately," he answered. *"You've become my muse."*

I tried to tell myself that his flattery was no different from my other mentors along the way, such as Suzy Thompson and Mary Jo Salter. But I was lying to myself, and I knew it. And my capacity to even pretend to be in denial completely disappeared when a few days later his messages became charged with sensuality: the succulent plums he got at the market, the tender flesh of the aubergines he prepared for lunch, the juice that dripped from the sweet, plump oranges.

I needed to set the record straight, to nip his innuendo-laden messages in the bud. But I was afraid of embarrassing him, afraid of hurting our relationship. And I couldn't risk that. Not after the way he'd offered to help me. Not after the way I'd begun to depend on his feedback. But I kept all of this to myself; I didn't tell Olivia, Dr. Invicta, and certainly not Liam, who was as jealous as ever.

He came over the morning I interviewed people for the empty room, ostensibly to help me take care of some household logistics, though I was fairly certain he just wanted to make sure I wasn't considering any men. While I interviewed the first four people—all young women— Liam attended to a series of DIY projects I had been putting off. At noon we convened in the kitchen to make sandwiches.

"Old boy Al croaked yet?"

I couldn't help but laugh. "When are you going to let that go?"

"When you stop walking around with stars in your eyes. *Alistair*," he swooned in falsetto. "*Did you remember to take your Viagra?*"

I swatted him with a tea towel right as the doorbell rang. "She's early," I said, licking mayonnaise from my fingers and going down the hall to open the door.

The final candidate was a Swiss yoga teacher named Beatrice, who called herself Shanti. She floated into the apartment in a cloud of sandalwood, her billowing white jumpsuit lending additional ethereality to her curious appearance. Her skin was almost translucent, and her hair was white-blonde. Were it not for her piercing blue eyes, and the dark mole on her cheek, perfectly round with a long hair growing out of the center, she might have passed for albino.

Liam looked surprised at her ghostly appearance as I introduced them briefly before taking her to the bedroom.

Shanti had described herself as quiet and reserved in her inquiry, and she proved herself to be as much, going from dresser to desk to bed without a word. Then she poked the mattress with her fingers. "I'm particular. May I?"

"Test it out," I said. "I'll leave you alone for a few minutes to look around."

"She's an odd bird," Liam whispered when I joined him in the kitchen, where he was making coffee.

"Shhhhh!" I giggled, holding my finger to my lips.

Shanti appeared in the doorway. "The bed is fine," she said. "There's just one problem."

Liam and I followed her down the hallway.

"Mold," she said, pointing at the tub, her bony arm showing through the thin cotton of her sleeve.

It was a small, black patch, growing in the far corner, the likes of which I had lived with many times over the years. Agatha hadn't been bothered by it, either, at least not by the time she left. But mold could grow quickly. *Like irritation*, I thought, eying Liam.

"The silicone needs to be redone," Liam said.

"Can you have it done before the end of the month?" Shanti asked him, before turning to me. "I'll take the room if you can get that cleaned up."

Liam looked at me. "Don't worry, sweetheart. I'll take care of it." Then he turned to Shanti. "Happy to do it."

A sense of unease with this whole rapid-fire arrangement grumbled in my stomach. I had already decided that Shanti would be the winning candidate—the others had been a bit too garrulous for my liking—but Liam didn't know that, and it annoyed me the way he just took over.

When Shanti was gone, Liam said, "I can come by this weekend to do the bathroom. I'll do both of them, if you like."

"One is fine," I said, torn between gratitude and weariness. It was a gift he was offering, free labor for a task that at Geneva prices would definitely set me back a couple of hundred. But would it really be free?

He studied my face, aware that I was miffed. "You know I'd do anything for you?"

I suddenly felt guilty about my petulance. "Thanks for your help. I do really appreciate it."

Then he stepped toward me and put his hands on my shoulders. Out of the corner of my eye, I could see my rumpled bed, the cats lying on it, entangled in a sunbeam. I could smell Liam, that delicious blend of soap and mountain. I had a dizzying spin of thoughts; the mold, the money, the bed, the cats, who were now licking each other dedicatedly. I kissed him and led him to the bed, knowing somewhere inside me that this would be the last time.

CHAPTER TWENTY-FOUR

Paris, France 2003

The summer of my thirty-fourth birthday, I got an email from Fran, whom I hadn't seen since she moved to Saudi Arabia right after sixth grade. *"I'm not sure I have the right Kristin Duncombe,"* she wrote. *"Is this the same one that lived in the Ivory Coast from 1979 to 1983?"*

I answered immediately.

"Yes! Amazing to hear from you after all these years!" I wrote, before peppering my message with questions about how her life had evolved since our last sight of each other, roughly twenty years earlier. I knew that she had also been revealed as one of Mr. Mulcahy's victims during the fallout and the investigation, but we had never discussed it. I assumed we would now, but I didn't want to leap right into that story, as though it was the only thing that mattered. So I added, *"As for me, I've been living in Paris for two years now, and I love it here. I'm married and have a four-year-old daughter, Carmen. I'm on my own with her a lot because my husband travels for work, but I don't mind because we had a major crisis two years ago when ..."*

I hesitated, then deleted any mention of our crisis. The first year in Paris was colored by the recovery from our split, but what really defined my life now was the work I had been doing to get on my feet, build my own solid existence. *"I trained to be a psychotherapist in New Orleans, and I have been building a private practice here. I work with a lot of expats—big surprise, eh?—and I love being self-employed. OK, enough about me. Tell me about you!"*

I attached some photos of Carmen to the email and hit SEND. Within a minute, she answered.

"I'm sorry to not be chatty, but there's something urgent to address first. Read this and get back to me. I will be waiting at the computer."

I clicked the link she forwarded.

Ex Foreign Service Officer Arrested for Child Rape

At first, my eyes could not make sense of what they were seeing. I looked at the photo and I read the headline again.

Oh my God.

It was Mr. Mulcahy.

His hair had gone white, but he had the same drooly lip, the same bulging eyes.

It was him.

Twenty-two years had passed since Mr. Mulcahy was lifted out of my life. Twenty-two years since he last imposed himself on me.

Twenty-two years!

But I remembered as though it was yesterday: the rustling of clothing, his hands plump and pale, his heavy breath hot on my shoulder. One sight of that photo and time peeled back to Rose's house, the car, the swimming pool.

I felt lightheaded, as if all the air had been sucked from the room, sealing me in with nothing but the memory. I don't know how much time passed—twenty seconds? twenty minutes?—before I climbed into bed, pulling the covers over my head. I wanted to howl, but my throat had tightened. A single thought thrummed through my head, over and over: *twenty-two years later, an eight-year-old girl paid.*

The days that followed were like driving through heavy fog. Fran and I wrote back and forth. She told me she had stumbled across the headline while in line at the grocery store. She lived an hour from where the rape took place, so she called information for Rose's number. Hardly a joyous reunion, Rose was completely shattered. The eight-year-old victim was her niece, the daughter of her older sister, Meg, my teenage idol of the cool T-shirts and albums.

Mr. Mulcahy raped his granddaughter.

Devastated. Devastating. Devastation.

In a sick repeat of what took place in Abidjan so many years ago, one by one, other children came forward. And not only children, but also adults he'd abused when they were children.

One week after getting the news of Mr. Mulcahy's arrest, I spoke to Rose for the first time since my parents forbade me to speak to her ever again. My hands trembled so badly I had trouble punching in the numbers. When her voice came through the receiver, a voice that had taken the same raspy quality as her mom's, we laughed, and then cried, great gulping sobs. We were closer to the age our mothers had been at that time, but it was as though we were still children. We were doused in injury, the crimes of Rose's father so vast, the abandonment by the State Department so glaring.

"Now I know why I never heard from any of my friends again," Rose sobbed. "All these years I thought it was because of something I had done. I am so sorry, so, so, sorry. I was his bait. He used me as bait."

I tried to console her. It wasn't *her* fault; she was the biggest victim of all, condemned to live under the same roof as a pedophile, and made to pay for his depravity by losing her entire community. And I still didn't know the answer to the most unbearable question. "Did he do it to you, too?"

"I don't know," she wept. Her voice sounded small. "I wet my bed the night he was arrested."

I suddenly remembered that day, long ago, in the changing room at the pool of the Hotel Ivoire. *Can I tell you a secret? I wet my bed last night. I don't want my dad to find out. He gets super angry about stuff like that.*

We listened to each other cry. Then I heard the *swiip* of a tissue being pulled from the box. Rose blew her nose and said, "I keep thinking about when my daughter was little. He always wanted to babysit. I was never comfortable with it, and rarely allowed it, but that was because he used the belt on us—"

"What?"

"You didn't know; no one did, outside of the family. My dad had a nasty temper. He mostly did it to my sister, but we all feared it could happen to us."

I was less shocked by this piece of information than I was by the fact I was shocked at all. Why should this surprise me? But despite everything, I still had an image of Mr. Mulcahy as a jolly jokester, not an angry man with a belt.

"By the time I met you, it was mostly a thing of the past. But it was always in the backdrop. Remember those dreams I had about a mean man whacking me? I didn't think of it as my dad. It just seems so obvious now. And my mother is distraught. Her whole life was built around his lies. And now she's realizing all the people that lied to her, over time, to protect him."

My mind flashed to my mother crying. *How could this have happened? How could we have missed all these clues? It seems so obvious now.*

"Like that day in Abidjan when the ambassador came over to tell my dad he had to leave, the two of them told my mother he was getting some big promotion," Rose continued. "And when we got back to Washington, it was so hard for me and my mom. We'd had no time to prepare mentally, and logistically it was a nightmare, trying to find a house, a school …" Her voice trailed off for a moment, and then she said, "Meanwhile that monster I used to call my father spent every Friday 'in New York' where he had this 'super important consultancy.' You know what it was? His 'punishment.' Some treatment program for sex offenders."

"I can't even—"

"Do you have a therapist?"

"Not right now—"

"Get one. And send the bill to the State Department."

"I kind of had a … a … nervous breakdown," I said, clearing my throat uncomfortably. "When I was twenty-two. Living in Seattle. It's a long story, but the State Department already gave me twenty thousand dollars for therapy."

"They paid you off?"

"No, it was for therapy—"

"Twenty thousand dollars. For therapy." She sounded outraged. "Was that *enough?*"

The incongruence between what had happened and the "compensation" they had offered me was suddenly glaring. "It got used up quickly. I had a backlog of therapy bills to pay, and then I bought myself a few things." My Doc Martens came into focus, as did the second-hand car I bought, the first car I ever owned, the car that gave me my taste for road-tripping. "My therapist, Janet, kept telling me I shouldn't feel lucky for getting that money. And I kept telling her I had done nothing to earn it."

"You did nothing to deserve my father's abuse," Rose sobbed. "None of us did. That he could walk free is criminal. But there's going to be a trial now. You're going to hear from the investigator. Is that OK?"

In the dark recesses of my brain, I suddenly heard Mr. Hornsby's voice. *How deep inside your vagina did Mr. Mulcahy insert his finger? You can put your finger up my sleeve.*

So many years later, that memory still held so much power that my stomach lurched.

But I wasn't that twelve-year-old girl anymore, and I wasn't that twenty-two-year-old girl, either. I was a thirty-four-year-old woman, mother to a daughter, who knew rationally that I had nothing to be ashamed of. The blame was squarely on Mr. Mulcahy and the people in power who silenced a traumatized community.

"Of course, it's OK. I'll do anything I can to help with the investigation."

By the time we hung up, I was drained. We promised to call each other again soon, but as the weeks passed, neither of us picked up the phone. Then Rose wrote.

"My father has provided a list of victims, and I'm on it. My heart is black with rage. I don't know how to go on, but I will, for my daughter."

In the weeks following this revelation, Rose went silent. Then she wrote again to say that she had bottomed out; her father's admission had unleashed a wave of traumatic memory, and she was receiving intensive therapy from a trauma specialist who was helping her make sense of memory repression.

"My therapist says it occurs unconsciously and spontaneously. It is how the brain organizes itself when something is too unbearable to face."

Similar to the true and false selves I would discuss with Dr. Invicta years later, Rose's brain had compartmentalized her father's abuse so efficiently that it had been moved to a nonconscious realm of her brain and sealed tight.

Until now.

I moved through my days on autopilot. I didn't dare cancel any of my therapy clients; I was still too new to private practice, still too inexperienced to feel safe rescheduling. What if they never came back? And anyway, it helped, sitting and listening to other people's problems. It was respite from the reliving of the Mulcahy chapter; the abuse, the fallout, and now, the guilt that none of us had done more to stop him. *Twenty-two years later, an eight-year-old girl paid.*

When I wasn't at work, I spent most of my time snuggled on the sofa with Carmen. We watched a lot of videos those days; it was so much easier to hold back the tears that way. But I couldn't contain them when I got the email from Rose, where she wrote: *"I've given your name to the detective in charge of the case. He's collecting depositions. You can't testify anymore—some bullshit about the statute of limitations—but every word will help lock my father away. And we need every word, because apparently, raping an eight-year-old girl isn't enough to lock him up forever."*

"Barnstable Police Department. How may I direct your call?"

"I have a telephone appointment with Sargent James Scotter. In the Sex Crimes Unit?"

"Just a moment."

"James Scotter."

"Sargent Scotter?" I repeated his name, taken aback by how much he sounded like JFK.

"Speaking. Is this … uhhh … "

Through the phone, on the other side of the ocean, I heard papers rustling. I imagined him going through a long list, trying to figure out which victim he was speaking to now. "This is Kristin Duncombe."

"Duncombe! Yes, sorry. I was waiting for your call. There are several people making a deposition long distance … No one else from Paris, though. Shall we get started?"

"Yes, please. But I wanted to clarify: I really can't testify? I'd happily fly—"

"You really can't. The statute of limitations has expired—"

"It's so … unfair." I felt like that twelve-year-old girl again, watching Mr. Hornsby come into the living room with his notebook, trepidation about what would happen next. But there was something else: I felt how my parents must have felt, being told that the case was closed, that there would be no recourse.

"I completely agree. And I've had this conversation too many times this week. But we'll work with what we have, all right? All the victim's statements, the depositions, they'll help send Mulcahy to jail."

For the record, Sargent Scotter asked my name, age, and relationship to the perpetrator. I felt oddly removed, as though I was talking about someone else, a client or someone I read about in the newspaper. Then he asked me for the story, and I started reciting the facts, as though from a checklist, like the tort claim I filled out twelve years earlier.

Sargent Scotter interrupted. "William Mulcahy was your father's colleague?"

"He was a diplomat, yes, at the US Embassy in the Ivory Coast. But my connection to him was through his daughter Rose. She was my best friend."

As I said those words, the reality of what I was talking about blinkered in my mind, like a fluorescent bulb coming to light: Two preteen girls, slow dancing with each other, "Too Much, Too Little, Too Late" playing on the stereo. Two preteen girls, giggling over so many dreams, about boys, and love, and how their lives might turn out. Two preteen girls, with huge, awful secrets.

Tears streamed down my face, but I didn't even realize I was crying until Sargent Scotter's voice broke into my reverie. "Breathe easy," he said. "Cry as much as you need to. We have time."

"It's just such a sad story," I wept. "It's unbearably sad."

"Yes, it is," Sargent Scotter said. "But you know what? It's going to be OK. *You're* going to be OK. Because it's never too late to tell your story, and get a better ending."

Barnstable, Massachusetts 2004

William Frances Mulcahy, age 79, was convicted of six counts of raping a child, and two counts of child sexual abuse. The court was aware of other depositions submitted by adults he had victimized as children, in the United States and overseas. Because of the statute of limitations, Mulcahy could not be tried on these counts.

He was sentenced to five to eight years of prison, without parole.

CHAPTER TWENTY-FIVE

Geneva, Switzerland 2018

Crumbs! You didn't get them all!" Shanti's shrill voice carried down the hallway from the kitchen. Then, Lorenzo's low, "Sorry," and the sound of sweeping.

Shanti had taken us prisoner, with her bossiness and her contamination phobia, and after a month of living together, I knew I had made a big mistake taking her on. She opened the doors of the bathrooms with her elbows, afraid to touch the handles, and she burned some purifying leaf in her room to "create a barrier of disinfection" between her space and the rest of the house.

"I can't stand her!" I moaned to Olivia later that evening after Lorenzo had gone to Tano's. Shanti was out with friends, and I was feeling relaxed for the first time in weeks.

"Can't you ask her to leave?" Olivia giggled, popping an olive in her mouth while I checked the vegetarian lasagna bubbling in the oven. "Otherwise, you'll be living like a hostage in your own home."

"*Will be?* Already am. And yes, I can ask her to leave." I took the food from the oven and turned to Olivia. "But let's change the subject.

Now that she's out of my hair for a few hours, I don't want to spend that time thinking about her."

Olivia laughed and started telling me about a new dating site she signed up on. I listened and nodded along as she showed me all the new men she had matched with. Then I said, "Ugh."

"Are you OK?"

"No. I mean, yes. But there's something I want to talk to you about."

"Do tell," Olivia said, topping up our glasses.

"Remember the deal with Alistair Grand? That he'd help me with some editing?"

She nodded, and I continued speaking while I dished up our plates. "It's been a huge help," I said. "The manuscript is over a hundred pages long now, and it's solid. Coherent. And it's thanks to his comments and suggestions."

"That's good," she said, taking a fork and stealing a bite from one of the plates.

"It is, yes…"

"This is so good." She took another bite. "Remind me where he lives?"

"London. But he's in Montreux right now, for his goddaughter's wedding. We're scheduled to meet at the end of the week for that drink we'd agreed to, in exchange for his editorial help."

"Cool," she said, taking her plate and nodding towards the living room. "Can we go eat?"

We went down the hallway together, balancing plates, wine glasses and bottle, and the salt and pepper mills. When we were seated, I took a deep breath. "There's more to the Alistair Grand story." I started at the beginning, going back to my phone to read some of his messages out loud. "And now I'm supposed to meet him in ten days. And …" I closed my eyes.

"And what?"

"And I don't want to go."

"So, don't! Not if he's been saying things that make you feel uncomfortable."

"I wasn't actually uncomfortable. But then he sent me this." I pulled up his most recent email and handed Olivia the phone. I watched her face as she read the passage he'd copied and pasted from a book he was reading. Something about an older man devouring the silky, wet flesh of a ripe peach.

"*Eeeeeewwww!*" Olivia threw my phone to the sofa as though it were contaminated. "That is disgusting! Do not go meet that man in Montreux!"

She stabbed at her lasagna with her fork, and tomato sauce shot from its surface like lava. I knew she was right; the reunion was ruined. I wanted to talk about first-person, and character development, and narrative arc, but all I could think about was Alistair Grand obsessing about peaches.

"I don't know how to get out of it."

Olivia looked at me like I was crazy. "Have you lost your mind? You hit REPLY, and write, 'Thanks for grossing me out you old creep,' and then you block him."

She looked so aghast I had to laugh.

"I swear to God, I'm going to go to the station and prevent you from getting on that train if you do not come to your senses. What does your shrink say?"

"I haven't told her yet."

"Promise me you will not go see that pedophile."

"He's not a pedophile!"

"He is thirty years older than you!"

"Olivia, he's not a pedophile, because I am not a child!"

Olivia changed the subject, but I barely heard a word she said. My own words were ringing in my ears. *I am not a child.*

I had only recently realized that I had been stuck in a childlike identity all these years, and now, just like that, I also knew that I had grown up. *I am not a child.*

That night I fell into a fast sleep, and had a terrible dream about eating a watermelon. It was so delicious and juicy, and it didn't even have seeds. At least, not the black ones. Just those little white baby seeds. But as I bit into another chunk, the seeds moved—maggots!

I woke with a start, feeling sick. That scenario hadn't come out of nowhere; it was straight from the annals of childhood, an actual thing that had happened to Mrs. Hornsby, wife of the security officer, mother of the little boy I babysat in Abidjan. I could remember as though it were yesterday, standing in their kitchen, the sound of the flies trapped between the case of the light fixture and the flickering fluorescent bulb, while she opened cupboard doors to point out the snacks I could have while they were out. *And I had planned to leave you the most wonderful watermelon, but …!*

Insomnia denied me the respite of unconsciousness, and I crept to the kitchen, praying that Shanti wasn't awake doing some irritating purification ritual as she was prone to in the early morning. Since she had moved in, I had stopped working on my manuscript in that beloved early morning space; hearing her rattling around in the kitchen made me so annoyed I couldn't focus. Instead, I now took early morning walks, and because Lorenzo had slept at his dad's last night and I didn't need to see him off to school, I got dressed and left the house.

I took a long walk around the lake, thinking about last night's conversation with Olivia. Suddenly my phone rang. It was Dr. Invicta, calling to say she had an out-of-town emergency and was cancelling all sessions that week. Before we hung up, I asked if I could quickly tell her about the dream I'd had. "I'd like to hear your interpretation."

"I'd rather hear yours," she countered. "Tell me what it means to you."

"I guess the worms stand for sex, or men, or Alistair Grand … something like that."

"Could the worms be you?"

"*Me?* I thought I was the watermelon." I thought about it for a moment. "Though same difference, I guess. It's all rotten fruit."

"We've been trying to understand the duality in you. There is the high-functioning, secure part of you. That's the watermelon. And then there's the part defined by this negative self-image, fused with being pleasing to men. The part that always says there's something wrong with you that only a man's desire can disprove. That's the worms. We'll continue to explore this duality going forward, but I'm going to have to get off the phone now."

"Thank you, Dr. Invicta," I said. "I'll see you in a week."

"Just one last thing before we hang up."

"Yes?"

"Take care of yourself, my dear. You're not rotten, I promise."

I tried to put the conversations with Olivia and Dr. Invicta out of my mind, just for twenty-four hours, to let it all sink in and simmer before I decided about whether to meet Alistair Grand in Montreux. It was hard to keep my thoughts away from it, though, because he kept sending me emails about how much he was looking forward to catching up in person. It was already Wednesday, and we were supposed to meet that Saturday. I knew I had to decide.

Was it the pressure of the decision or the fumes of Shanti's latest purification ritual? I wasn't sure, but a migraine took hold and caused such pounding behind my eyes that I was forced to clear the rest of my day. I took a migraine tablet, the strong kind that made me sleepy, and filled a Ziploc bag with ice. Then I got into bed and positioned it over my forehead and eyes, tucked my hands into the elastic waistband of my pants, and tried to concentrate on the rise and fall of my breath. I just wanted to stop the pain.

I was thinking about being on the train to Montreux as I floated off into that hazy zone between sleep and wakefulness ...

Alistair texts you as the train pulls into the station in Montreux: he is already at the bar, waiting. Your legs feel heavy, walking from the station to the hotel. You stop in the bar's doorway, and for a few minutes, watch him from a distance, sitting by the window. Just beyond him, Lac Leman sparkles, a diamond collar to the Alps. He spots you and as you approach, he stands up awkwardly, knocking the table, sloshing his glass of water. He gestures to the view. "It's distracting," he says, shaking your hand and then pulling you in for a kiss on each cheek. He smells of vodka and cream.

"White Russian?" He waves for the waiter. "I'm on my second."

When your drink comes, you toss it down your throat and try to relax as the warm feeling seeps into your veins. You need another one, fast. Where's the waiter? You talk about the wedding he attended. You talk about his book tour. You talk about your manuscript and what happened to you when you were a kid. He gets emotional, says he wishes he had been there to protect you. Tells you he thinks the world of you.

He calls the waiter for more drinks; you are woozy, loose. You don't pull away when he takes your hand and brings it to his lips.

"Spend the night with me," he says. His eyes are liquid and pleading, and you want to bolt, to leap up so fast your chair falls over and run until you are out of the hotel and back on the train. Instead, you say, "I can't spend the night. But I can stay with you for a while."

And then the dominos fall. You watch him sign for the bar tab, watch how his puffy, freckled hand holds the pen. You know that hand will touch your flesh and you prepare yourself to get through it, walking to the elevator with him, heavy, slow, as though through quicksand. In the elevator he presses himself to you, parting your lips with his thick, coated tongue. He tastes of garlic and alcohol. The doors open and you follow him down the silent, carpeted hallway. He fumbles with the key. You can see he is nervous, but then you are in the room and the first thing you see are his slippers, fuzzy and worn ...

✳

I sat up, abruptly, the Ziploc bag falling to the floor and breaking open with a splash. The dream was so vivid, I could still see it, could see what came next: me, splayed open on the bed, Alistair Grand's jowled face coming at me, crazy with greed.

I swung my legs over the side of the bed and felt the shock of cold as my feet landed in the puddle of melted ice. I shuddered. *I cannot go through with this.*

You don't have to.

I don't want to.

You don't have to.

As I got up in search of a towel, shaking the water from my toes, I realized the headache was gone. I sopped up the water, but it wasn't the cold that was making me shiver. It was the knowledge that *I* didn't have to.

And I wouldn't.

CHAPTER TWENTY-SIX

Geneva, Switzerland 2018

I couldn't believe I had done it, but Dr. Invicta said, "You were ready. Ready to leap. Ready to reclaim your voice. Your NO. I am so proud of you."

"Thanks," I said, beaming. "I'm proud of me too. I felt so … *grown up.* Like I could do… anything. *Everything.* I even started having this fantasy of confronting Mr. Mulcahy." I laughed. "I was literally having this vision of walking the streets of Boston, with a flashlight, trying to find him."

"I don't follow. He's not in prison?"

"No! He got out after five years! Against his entire family's wishes. So they had him committed to an institution for sex offenders, to keep him off the streets. And he was supposed to be locked up there for the rest of his life. But two of the staff psychiatrists deemed him no longer dangerous and released him."

"Where is he now?"

"I don't know. They released him to a homeless shelter." I poured some water but didn't drink it. Dr. Invicta didn't say anything for a moment. Then she broke the silence.

"If you did find him, what would you say?"

I closed my eyes and tried to imagine the standoff, some type of verbal Krav Maga, but all that came to mind were the things I once loved and admired: Playing Twister. Going for ice cream. *Pizzillis.* Boat rides. *Fun.*

I opened my eyes. "I'd say, 'I looked up to you. The way you horsed around and teased me made me feel important. I wasn't used to being noticed the way you noticed me.'" My voice trembled. "'You tricked me,' is what I would say. 'You took my inherent trust in adults and confused it. Confused me. I was a child, and you stole my sense of safety, my innocence, any notion that my body was my own and not something I owed you. Owed men. You installed in me such an enormous capacity to suppress my instinct that I became my worst enemy, and I could not protect myself from the dangers of living in a world that has so many variations of predators like you.'"

"*Yes,*" Dr. Invicta said. "*Yes.* Mr. Mulcahy ended a part of your childhood years before you were ready. He sped up your sexual development, and it was unmanageable for you, psychologically. He forced a split in your psyche that you've been trying to close for so many years."

"Do you think I've managed?"

"What do *you* think?"

I thought about it for a moment. Since leaving my marriage, I had discovered that I *could* stand on my own two feet and manage those things that had once seemed daunting. I had made some big mistakes as I re-entered the dating world, but they had helped me get to this point.

"It's that hard to measure?" Dr. Invicta's voice cut into my thoughts.

"There's just something niggling at me. Something that feels like the next big step."

"What do you mean, you don't want me to do the bathtub for you? How will you do it?"

Liam was on the phone, annoyed. He had done an amazing job cleaning up the silicone in Shanti's bathroom, and had "offered" to do the same for the other bathroom. More like insisted, even though I told him I wanted to take care of it myself. I knew the strings that came with having him over to help me, but he had refused to take no for an answer. We were supposed to meet the next day, and mounting anxiety about seeing him had snapped me out of that old boundarylessness. "It's something *I* need to do, Liam. I need to step up my efforts to take care of things myself."

He didn't respond, and the silence stretched so long that I wondered if we had been disconnected. Then he spoke. "So, you're dumping me, for real. Is that it?"

"It's not—"

"Not what? Say it! 'I've used you up, Liam, so now you can be on your pitiful little way.'"

"That's not fair. And you're not even letting me speak."

"Got some other bloke already? Getting ready to fuck his brains out, are you?"

"I'm not breaking up with you for anyone." It felt so good to say that; not so long ago, I would have already been looking for the next man, using him as a parachute when I jumped. Now I didn't feel the need to do that. I cleared my throat, got up from my chair, and went to the window. Outside, a group of schoolchildren were being shepherded across the street.

"You expect me to believe that?"

"Well, it's the truth, so I hope you will," I said, returning to my chair and putting my feet up on the table.

"I don't believe a word you say."

"All the more reason for us to stop here, then."

"This is bullshit."

I was suddenly angry, and in one motion, put my feet on the floor and stood up. "You wanna know what's bullshit? The way you act like I'm obligated to you. I'm *allowed* to break up with you."

I waited for him to bark at me, but several beats of silence made me realize he was no longer there. He had hung up. I imagined him on his mountain, face beet red, slamming things around, probably feeling cheated by modern technology that the good old-fashioned slamming down of the receiver was no longer a thing. Unless of course we had just gotten cut off. Were that the case, he'd call back, and I held my phone in my hand, waiting for it to ring.

But it didn't.

It was over.

I sat there for a moment, letting it sink in. I felt many things, but mostly just a tremendous sense of relief. This is what it felt like to have boundaries, and to feel secure enough to enforce them. I'd done it with Alistair Grand, now I was doing it with Liam. My mind flashed to the bathtub; it would have been easier—in one way—to have just let Liam do the work for me. In another way, I would have had to pay with a currency that I was no longer using.

I scrolled through YouTube, looking for the perfect instructional video on applying silicone. I watched a few on how to scrape out the old gunk and seal in the new. *That's an apt metaphor*, I thought, as I plunked down in the bathtub and gouged at the mold, imagining it as the traumatic muck of the years.

Eventually, I got the black patch out, but it wasn't as easy as just excising the blemish. The chunks of yellowing rubber had come out fairly easily, but now there was a gaping disconnect between the tub and the wall, and squeezing in the silicone was not proving to be this effortless, pristine task, the way it had been for the guy in the video.

I took a deep breath and sat back on my heels. *You can do this.*

As I worked, I listened to the Christine Blasey Ford–Brett Kavanaugh hearings. I felt kindred to her, as if she was speaking for me. I had spent so much of my life afraid of men, never knowing who I was actually dealing with, realizing the mistake of trusting someone only when it was too late. I thought of Mulcahy, Nasser, Epstein, Weinstein, and so many others. And now this snivelling, belligerent Brett Kavanaugh, nominated by a man who gloated about "grabbing women by the pussy."

It was unbearable, listening to those patriarchal senators grilling Christine Blasey Ford about how could she possibly have constructed such a solid life if something "so traumatic" had happened to her?

What the fuck did they know about the duality women lived with?

Of course, she had built a successful life, you entitled morons, I thought, as I stabbed at the gunk. *If all the women who had been sexually abused were incapacitated, the whole world would have shut down a long time ago.*

I went back to scraping with renewed vigor. It wasn't enough to remove most of the mold; you had to scrape it clean. My mind swirled through my life, reconstructing the events that brought me to this moment. Mulcahy had sealed in all that poisonous self-loathing that set the stage for everything that followed. I'd tried to throw it up, drink it away, be the perfect girl so men would like me. So they wouldn't know how unimportant I felt, how powerless.

What might have been the course of my life if none of this had ever happened?

What if I had just told on Mulcahy, like Jenny Baxter did?

What if I had grown, and not shrunk, before Britney and her *slut slut slut?*

What if I had made it known that Dirk had cheated the system, and I wanted nothing to do with it?

What if I had pressed charges against Uday?

What if, all those years ago in New Orleans, when I was fresh-faced and twenty-six years old, *I* had made *Tano* choose?

Questions begat more questions, and my mind spun through all the answers, imagining a life that might have been *if … if … if …* I couldn't imagine who I might have been if none of those things had happened. And then I realized, I wouldn't have been me. I would have been someone else. And were I someone else, I wouldn't right now be squeezing out that final spurt of silicone, sitting back, and realizing, with joy: the joints were sealed!

Admittedly, my work wasn't pristine.

But it was done.

Thirty-six years had passed since the horrible truth about William Mulcahy was revealed. Twenty-six years since my nervous breakdown in Seattle. Twenty-one years since getting married and going off on a life I didn't want. Fifteen years since an eight-year-old girl was raped on Cape Cod because of the craven system that considered a terrible, perverted man to be more important than all the girls he victimized.

It had taken almost four decades, but something had finally shifted inside me; something about how I understood the world and my place in it. My mind travelled back to that day in Grand Bassam, when I was ten years old and Mr. Mulcahy molested me for the first time. I thought of my Snoopy bathing suit, how cool I felt when I wore it, and how I had gone home that evening and picked at the Snoopy logo, the very thing that made me love it so, until it unravelled completely. I never wore it again.

All I could hear now was Sargent Scotter's compassionate voice; it had been buried somewhere deep inside me, until now, when it came out to speak again:

It's never too late to tell your story, and get a better ending.

This time, I realized, I might even believe him.

I woke early, hours before sunrise, full of energy, even though I had slept so little. I crept to the kitchen to make coffee, revelling in the silence and the smell of silicone from yesterday's work. Then I went to my office—my beloved office—and pulled up my email.

The first message I saw was from Rose.

My father died today.
I thought you would want to know.

Dead? I put my hands on the desk to steady the spinning. *Mr. Mulcahy was dead?*

I had never actually contemplated this moment. It had never occurred to me that Mr. Mulcahy would *die*. And why was I crying? Wasn't this supposed to be like when the witch died in *The Wizard of Oz*? Shouldn't I be breaking out the champagne?

I got back into bed and stayed there for as long as I could, scrolling back through my exchanges with Rose, scrolling back over the years. One message stood out.

I can't go back, and I can't reconcile the damage. There are so many casualties because of him. Physical, mental, emotional … I feel like the only one I can't get closure on is my childhood fantasy of us being lifelong best friends, who went to college together, were at each other's weddings, knew each other's children.

I read those words over and over. *That* was it, that was why there was no jubilation, no *ding-dong, the child molester is dead*. Mr. Mulcahy's death couldn't bring back what he killed. Rose and I didn't get to be lifelong best friends, who went to college together, side by side through weddings and the raising of children.

We didn't get to, and we'd never get to.

We might still have a chance to rebuild a friendship, one that went beyond social media and the occasional painful email, in which we had to consider all that we'd lost. Geography and the demands of adult life had prevented us from doing much more than that, or maybe we had just been in too much pain.

There was no celebration; there was only grief.

I threw off the covers, trying to throw off this miserable feeling, and went, as I did every morning, to wake Lorenzo. He was deep in slumber, and I stood over him for just a moment, watching the rise and fall of his breath, the way his eyelashes curled on his perfect baby skin.

He was the age I was when the whole Mulcahy drama blew up.

I remembered Janet telling me to notice how young a twelve-year-old is, and then I remembered something Kenny used to say: *The best revenge is having a good life.*

I shook Lorenzo gently. "Wake up, sweetheart." He opened his big blue eyes, the same eyes as his sister, and smiled at me, and I knew one thing for sure: I had gotten my revenge many times over.

I was jotting some notes in my office that evening when I heard Shanti's voice coming from the kitchen. *Oh God, not again.* I could already tell, just by the tone, that she was harping at Lorenzo, and I cracked open the door to get a better listen.

"You need to get the vacuum cleaner out right now and get these crumbs off the floor, and then you need to wipe it down—"

I didn't hear the rest; the click of my boots covered her words as I stormed down the hallway. Lorenzo was standing there, knife poised over a jar of peanut butter, a piece of bread in his hand. Shanti had the mop bucket in hers. They both looked startled by my sudden arrival.

"What is the problem? Why are you harassing my son?"

Shanti opened her mouth, but Lorenzo beat her to it. "She's *mad*. About crumbs." He gestured to the floor with the knife, and a long drip of peanut butter fell to the tile. "Oops," he said, his eyes darting back to Shanti.

"He is *constantly* leaving a mess in the kitchen and—"

"I don't care!" I cut her off, anger snapping in my voice. "In fact, it's the very least of my concerns."

"Well, I find this unacceptable—"

"Then you'll need to find another place to live."

Shanti plonked the bucket down, hard. "I'll see about that when I'm ready!" Then she flounced out of the kitchen.

Lorenzo and I looked at each other. "Did you hear me, Mom? Right before you came, I told her she wasn't my mother, and I didn't have to listen to her!"

"I'm so proud of you for standing up to her." I put my arm around him.

"Is she gonna move out?"

"I bloody hope so." I went to the sink and held a glass under the faucet, enjoying the cool weight in my hand as it filled. I drank it down, and said, "Actually, she *is* moving out. I've decided. I'll give her until the end of the month. Now, can you wipe up the peanut butter?"

CHAPTER TWENTY-SEVEN

Geneva, Switzerland 2019

I ordered another coffee and pushed my chair back to catch the sliver of sun that had snuck in beneath the awning. I had taken the week off to work on the manuscript. I had a two-hundred-page draft that was still largely disjointed. Making sense of my story was still a work in progress, but I had written to Rose to ask for her blessing to tell the story of what happened with her father. I had been afraid of what that could stir up for her; the last thing I wanted to do was bring more pain to her life.

Whatever you write is fine by all of my family, she answered. *You must write your truth, and we believe that each of us has the right to express our personal issues in whatever constructive manner they choose. As for anonymity, you are free to use his name and mine as well. I live under no illusions. It is a part of my history, and trying to escape it doesn't help anyone. I'm glad you have been writing and hope it is cathartic for you. You write your truth, my friend, as goes the saying, "it will set you free." You don't ever have to worry about us. We face what he did head on… there are no candy-coated versions between any of us. I would be happy to read your manuscript. Let it out … put it in black and white so whomever reads may be helped.*

I had read her words dozens of times, and every time was like the first: a huge knot formed in my throat, and tears welled in my eyes. It felt like—

"Excuse me? Are you a writer? I've been sitting here for the last hour, watching you go through that stack of paper."

A man, forty-five or so, stood before me. He was nice looking, with a neatly trimmed beard and round glasses that lent an intellectual air to his appearance that was otherwise sporty, in his shiny Adidas track suit.

"Yes, I am."

"Writing a book?" He pulled up a chair and sat down.

"Yes, actually. I'm just beginning a first round of revision."

"Takes one to know one," he said, putting his hands behind his head, nodding with an appraising eye. "I'm a writer too. Essays, mostly, but I have a book up my sleeve. Been working on it—"

Don't ask what he thinks of you; what do you think of him?

"I'm sorry, but I was concentrating on something."

He looked confused.

"I'm working," I said. "I'm not here to socialize."

He stood up, flustered. "Right. Sorry, didn't mean to interrupt."

"No worries. Have a good day."

I watched him walk away. *Boundaries.* I still marveled at how my life had gotten easier now that I had no trouble setting them. Whenever I thought about all the years I wasn't able to do so, I grappled with this awful regret, similar to coming home after a weekend away and discovering someone had left a light on or the faucet dripping. *The loss, the loss.*

I turned back to my manuscript. Now that I was writing my story, the one that was transporting me into my happier ending, I could not bear to waste my resources. I wouldn't burn my light out anymore, or run my river dry. I still believed in love, and I still hoped that one day, I'd have a relationship again. But I would be the subject of my story from now on, never again the object of someone else's.

I thought often of my marriage—of the parts that were wonderful, and the parts that led to its demise. There was a particular memory I often returned to from the Great American Road Trip: arriving at the North Rim of the Grand Canyon, the more remote, less travelled side of it. There I stood at the edge of the canyon, flanked by my children. The view was stunning, a still life of colors and dimensions, peaks, valleys, and craggy edges, blending into each other. In that landscape, I saw my dying marriage: the depth and the beauty, and that, ultimately, it was unbridgeable.

My sorrow was as vast as the Grand Canyon.

And yet, I was grateful. Would I have found the happy ending to my story if there hadn't been something so glaring between Tano and me that it forced me to look at it, steadily, over the course of twenty years? I asked myself now, why did I ever expect Tano to be different, to accommodate what mattered to me? Why should he have, I finally realized, when that absolute position helped him make sense of his own life? I wasn't wrong for having wished it to be different, but I was crazy to have ever thought I could pry him off of that principle he was married to long before he ever married me.

As he once said, I always knew who he was.

And now I knew who I was, too.

It was a brave new world to be all grown up, standing on my two fully adult feet, in Geneva, Switzerland. The irony didn't escape me, that I arrived in neutral territory when I couldn't stay neutral any longer. I thought a lot about the Great American Road Trip of the summer of 2016. Sometimes it even entered my dreams, and when I woke, I had this feeling of being brave, out on the open road.

There was one dream in particular that was recurrent: I am at a gas station somewhere in America. I have just filled the tank, the children are buckled in, and we're ready to go.

Suddenly, Dennis the trucker pulls up.

"I got you some maps!" he says, jumping from the cab, crossing the station in wide strides. "I'll show you the route!"

He hands me a pen and tells me to write it down, and I pretend to scribble while he dictates a complicated series of detours and back roads. He won't stop talking, not even to take a breath, and finally I shout, "Enough!"

I always wake from this dream gasping, and one time, I actually started digging for a pen. But quickly now, my eyes make sense of the shapes in the dark room, and I remember: I know where I am.

I know where I'm going.

And I don't need any directions at all.

AUTHOR'S NOTE

OBJECT is a book about *complex* trauma, which describes arrested emotional development as a result of ongoing and repeated traumatic experiences that took place during childhood. "Fight, flight, or freeze" are terms that have become well recognized as characteristic responses to acute traumatic incidences. Less well recognized is "fawning," which refers to appeasing the other by being agreeable, non-confrontive, and compliant. Though fawning may appear to be "simple" people-pleasing, for survivors of sexual abuse it must be understood as a complex mechanism of self-defense. In the text of OBJECT, I am fawning when I describe "getting through" situations with men, by agreeing to physical and emotional arrangements that I did not actually want. In real time, fawning is a coping mechanism that staves off intense fears of abandonment or punishment, but it is also the self-defeating behavioral element, in my case, that led to the repeated trauma reenactments that characterized so many of my relationships with men.

Every woman I know, without exception, has experienced some form of sexual harassment or abuse. Fear of sexual assault, and dealing with the sequelae of aggression, is universal to the female experience. Also universal to the female experience is living under the pressure of constant sexual objectification. I wrote this book for my own healing and hopefully to help others with theirs.

If OBJECT resonated with you, and you would like to go further with additional reading, the following are some books – among many important titles - that I consider particularly accessible and useful:

- *Women and Desire: Beyond Wanting to be Wanted* by Polly Young Eisendrath
- *Believing Me: Healing from Narcissistic Abuse and Complex Trauma* by Ingrid Clayton
- *Complex PTSD: from Surviving to Thriving: A Guide and Map for Recovering from Childhood Trauma* by Pete Walker
- *The Unexpected Joy of Being Single and The Unexpected Joy of Being Sober* by Catherine Gray

ACKNOWLEDGMENTS

There is no adequate way to acknowledge Rose Mulcahy, and all she endured at the hands of her father and the community that abandoned her. She has been incredibly brave in her unwavering support that I tell the story of what happened to us. Thank you, Rose, from the bottom of my heart.

Many thanks and all my gratitude also go to Francesca Maffei, who had a much larger presence in my life in Abidjan than what this text reflects. This is due to my limitations as a writer and not a dearth of friendship.

Thank you to Lizzie Harwood, the only person who knew I was writing OBJECT for several tentative years, when I would periodically scribble out a paragraph and send it to her. She always responded with, "You have GOT to tell this story." Without her cheerleading I might not have dared. She was the first reader and editor of the original draft, and her belief in the book, and in my right to tell the story, gave me the confidence I needed to press on.

Thanks to Meg Bortin, who read multiple drafts of the book, and whose belief in its importance – and many an amazing home-cooked meal and late night dance session -- kept the wind behind my sails.

Thanks to my dear friend Kathleen Connors Bouchaud, who has encouraged and championed my writing from the very first pages of Trailing.

Thanks to the community of writers and readers that have provided invaluable feedback as I brought this book to life: Samantha Verant, Jennie Goutet, Jenna Land Free, Joelie Key Tissot, Caroline Leavitt, Laura Silverman, Michelle Hazen, Miranda Lukatch, Tenyia Lee, Catriona Turner, Jo Parfitt, Mariam Navaid Ottimofiore, Susan Blumberg-Kason, Caroline Harfield-Palany, Penny Trupe, Laura Michalek, Kelly McDonald, Wood Graham, and Patti Meyer.

I am incredibly grateful for the army of women who over the years have been my sounding boards, go-to's, life-partners, and best friends. Wendy Jacobs, Lisa Jordan, Aimee Pavitt, Hiba Samawi, Stephanie Duncombe, and Lesley Gramaglia were my lifelines during the Geneva years (and counting!). Ana Godinho was there in the early days and our relationship provided much fodder for my own self-discovery. Melissa Halligan Fraser deserves special mention for holding my hand and letting me drive her car one afternoon when I had a panic attack about taking my kids on the Great American Road Trip, when I hadn't driven a car in fifteen years. Christina Martin also deserves special mention for being the only one from the shared household we miss. Teresa Au, Julia Scott, Justine DuPlessis-Nelson, Julie Stilwell, Jessica Lynch, Malini Morzaria, Sharon Korman, Susan Clark, Kim Komer Mousseron, Rosamund Lewis, and Celine Esquenet. Thank you for being there.

Huge thanks to Polly Young-Eisendrath, whose book WOMEN AND DESIRE changed my life, by introducing me to the concept of being the subject of my own life, versus the object of someone else's.

Many thanks to Carole Bach, for all of her support.

Thanks also go to "detective" MPG, for teaching me how to fight my way out of objectification.

I want to acknowledge with gratitude the many good parts of my life with Tano, and express my sorrow for the things we just could not get beyond.

Thanks also to my mother and father for their support in my telling a story that brought pain to our family. My father died before I finished writing the first draft. My only consolation is that when I first started writing, I wondered how I would cope with him reading the sex scenes. His sudden departure took care of that, and I am only joking around about this because I know it would make him laugh.

Last, but never least, huge thanks and all my love goes to my children, Carmen and Lorenzo, the beating heart behind everything I do.

✳

LEAVE A REVIEW

I am grateful to every reader that takes the time to leave a review on Amazon. The more a book is reviewed, the more it becomes visible. Raising awareness is a critical component of ending rape culture; please help me spread the word about my story, by reviewing and by sharing with anyone you think might benefit from reading it. Thank you so much.

ABOUT THE AUTHOR

Kristin Louise Duncombe is an American therapist, life coach, and writer. She is the author of TRAILING: A Memoir and FIVE FLIGHTS UP: Sex, Love, and Family (from Paris to Lyon). She lives in Paris, France.

For more information or to get in touch, please visit her website at www.kristinduncombe.com

www.ingramcontent.com/pod-product-compliance
Lightning Source LLC
Chambersburg PA
CBHW051317130726
47987CB00004B/1840